ESSENTIAL SEAFOOD COOKBOOK

Essential Seafood Cookbook

CLASSIC RECIPES MADE SIMPLE

TERRI DIEN

FOREWORD BY CHEF MIA CHAMBERS

PHOTOGRAPHY BY DARREN MUIR

ROCKRIDGE PRESS

For general information on our other products and services or to obtain technical support, please contact our Customer Care Department within the United States at (866) 744-2665, or outside the United States at (510) 253-0500.

Rockridge Press publishes its books in a variety of electronic and print formats. Some content that appears in print may not be available in electronic books, and vice versa.

Interior and Cover Designer: Diana Haas
Art Producer: Megan Baggott
Editor: Daniel Grogan
Production Editor: Mia Moran
Photography © 2020 Darren Muir
Author photo by Carolyn Shek

ISBN: Print 978-1-64152-918-1 | eBook 978-1-64152-919-8
R0

To Mr. B, my better half

CONTENTS

FOREWORD BY CHEF MIA CHAMBERS X

INTRODUCTION XI

CHAPTER 1: WONDERFUL SEAFOOD 1

CHAPTER 2: BREAKFAST AND BRUNCH 15

Smoked Salmon Benedict 16

Shrimp Omelets 18

Smoked Mackerel Kedgeree 20

Hangtown Fry 22

Crab Strata with Pimentos
and Cheese 24

Salmon Hash with Fried Eggs 26

Smoked Trout and Bacon
Cornmeal Waffles 27

Smoked Salmon with Baked Eggs
in Avocados 28

Tuna and Tomato Frittata 29

Chilaquiles with Sautéed Shrimp 30

CHAPTER 3: APPETIZERS AND SALADS 33

Classic Crab Cakes 34

Shrimp Louie 35

Seared Ahi Tuna Niçoise Salad 36

Crab Potstickers 38

Layered California Sushi Dip 40

Shrimp and Papaya Salad 42

Salmon Mousse 43

Ceviche 45

Shrimp and Orzo Salad 46

Crab Rangoons 47

Clams Casino 48

Smoked Trout and Apple Salad 50

Smoked Salmon Deviled Eggs 51

Chinese Shrimp Toast 52

Summer Rolls 54

CHAPTER 4: SOUPS AND SANDWICHES 57

Quick and Easy Oyster Po' Boys 58

New England Clam Chowder 60

Crab Bisque 62

Classic Creole Shrimp Gumbo 64

Open-Faced Tuna Melts 66

Smoked Oyster Soup 67

Spicy Thai Coconut Shrimp Soup 68

Lobster Roll 69

Salmon Burgers 71

Cioppino 73

Bouillabaisse 75

Shrimp Banh Mi Sandwiches 77

Sardine and Pimento Bocadillos 79

Pan Bagnat (Provençal Tuna Sandwiches) 81

Trout Hand Pies 82

CHAPTER 5: ENTRÉES 85

Classic British Fish and Chips 86

Spicy Fideos with Mussels 38

Bang Bang Shrimp in Lettuce Cups 90

Broiled Shrimp Scampi with Crumbled Bacon 91

Chilean Sea Bass with Roasted Lemons and Fresh Herbs 92

Seafood Paella 94

Spaghetti with Clams 96

Lowcountry Boil 98

Cajun Catfish and Spinach Stew 99

Tuna Noodle Casserole 100

Fish Tacos with Pickled Vegetables 102

Fried Calamari with Rustic Tomato Sauce 104

Salmon Teriyaki 106

Sole Meunière 107

Blackened Catfish 108

Steamed Mussels with White Wine and Fennel 110

Scallop and Clam Pan Roast 111

Seared Scallops with Pineapple Beurre Blanc 112

Thai-Spiced Salmon Fillet en Papillote 114

Oysters Rockefeller 116

Macadamia-Crusted Mahi-Mahi 118

Roasted Salmon with Lemon-Garlic Butter 119

Fried Sardines with Gremolata 121

Broiled Halibut with Lemon-Herb Persillade 123

Grilled Tuna Steaks with Wasabi Butter 125

Cod in Spiced Tomato
Curry 126

Red Snapper Veracruz 127

Pistachio-Crusted Tuna and
Lentil Salad 128

Grilled Shrimp Kabobs with
Pesto Sauce 130

Drunken Crab with Garlic
Fried Rice 132

Grilled Mackerel with Dukkah
and Lemon 134

Jamaican Jerk Tilapia with
Coconut Rice 136

Roasted Sardines with Red Peppers
and Onions 138

Miso-Lacquered Black Cod 139

Lobster Mac and Cheese 140

MEASUREMENTS AND CONVERSIONS 143
RESOURCES 144
GLOSSARY 145
REFERENCES 148
INDEX 150

FOREWORD

Seafood cookbooks can be intimidating, but this one, dedicated to the home chef, is sophisticated yet unpretentious, and very rewarding. Most of us want to spend time with our family and friends by nourishing them with something fabulous for dinner rather than spending hours searching for recipes or navigating complicated instructions. These recipes are written for what people really want: simple, creative, approachable techniques. Terri has dedicated the past 15 years to teaching hands-on cooking classes to home cooks, and in the process she has learned their habits and developed effective ways to teach them. Nobody knows *how* we cook at home as well as *what* we really want from a cookbook better than Terri!

I first met Terri as she was just graduating from culinary school and interning for me at Draeger's Cooking School. We had much in common—both home cooks who decided to follow their passion for cooking and make a scary career change. It's been my great pleasure to watch Terri blossom from a hardworking intern into a trusted colleague and dear friend.

Terri is an excellent teacher who shares her enthusiasm for cooking with a great sense of humor and engaging style. Look forward to not only well-written, easy-to-follow recipes but also lots of great substitution ideas to spark your creativity. You're in the best of hands for guidance through the recipes you've always wanted to try!

CHEF MIA CHAMBERS
January 2020

INTRODUCTION

I LOVE SEAFOOD. It's all so delicious! Growing up, my favorite dishes were tuna fish on toasted bagels, red clam chowder, and my mom's steamed fish with ginger oil. In my college years, even when I was flat broke, I still found ways to enjoy seafood—even if it was just adding a can of salmon or some smoked oysters to a salad.

As a chef instructor, I learned that the best recipes are the simple ones that celebrate the fish as it is. In this book you'll find different cuisines to experiment with and techniques to make you more confident in cooking seafood. Use this book as an extended cooking lesson, and soon you'll be creating signature dishes of your own.

> *"Fish, to taste right, must swim three times—*
> *in water, in butter, and in wine."* –**Polish proverb**

Thai-Spiced Salmon Fillet en Papillote, page 114

CHAPTER 1

WONDERFUL SEAFOOD

SEAFOOD AND HEALTH:

While seafood can certainly be a decadent treat for special occasions, there are also many benefits in consuming it on a regular basis. Here are a few of them:

- Eating more fish and seafood regularly can reduce the risk of obesity. Both fish and seafood are low in calories and saturated fat but high in protein and healthy fats, which means they will keep you fuller longer. If you're being calorie conscious, get your daily intake by eating more fish without going overboard on butter or oil.

- The American Heart Association recommends all healthy adults consume fish at least twice a week to prevent cardiovascular diseases such as stroke. The high levels of HDL (the "good" cholesterol) in fish can help lower overall cholesterol levels.

- Fish is a brain booster! Researchers from the Ronald Reagan UCLA Medical Center have found that consumption of baked or broiled fish on a regular basis is linked to higher functionality in areas of the brain that are responsible for comprehension and recollection in adults. Eating fish can also prevent plaque buildup in the brain, which is believed to be one of the causes of Alzheimer's disease.

- Consuming fish can have a significant impact on mental health. Fatty fish such as salmon contains high levels of protein, selenium, and omega-3s, which can help balance mood and lower the risk of depression.

A common concern people have with seafood and fish is the potential for high levels of mercury. Mercury is toxic to a child's developing brain and nervous system, so the Food and Drug Administration warns women who may become pregnant, are pregnant, or are nursing to avoid fish with high amounts of mercury. A general rule of thumb is that the larger (and more predatory) the fish, the higher the mercury, and since mercury is present in fish, the concentrations increase the more a fish eats other fish.

According to the National Resources Defense Council, some fish and seafood that are low in mercury are catfish, clams, crab, salmon, sardines, shrimp, tilapia, and freshwater trout. Some fish that contain higher levels of mercury are grouper, king mackerel, swordfish, orange roughy, and bigeye and ahi tuna. As with most things, eating fish high in mercury is generally okay as long as it is consumed sparingly.

FRESHWATER VS. SALTWATER

The primary difference between freshwater fish and saltwater fish is the flavor. Saltwater fish have a brinier taste but, despite their environment, do not carry high levels of sodium due to a circulatory system that keeps them from absorbing the salt in ocean water. Saltwater fish have a variety of textures and flavors, whereas freshwater fish have a milder flavor with smaller flakes and bones. You may notice that freshwater fish are more heavily prepared, including marinating, frying, and adding lots of complementary spices and sauces, while saltwater fish are usually more simply made with very few additional aromatics.

SUSTAINABILITY

Social awareness of the fishing industry, including the supply levels and environments fish are raised in, has brought to light destructive fishing methods that compromise and threaten the ocean's ecosystems. As consumers, we have a responsibility to be mindful when purchasing seafood and to make sustainability a priority.

FARMED VS. WILD

Farm raising fish, or aquaculture, is a method by which fish are cultivated, ensuring that populations of certain species will not dwindle. As such, aquaculture can have a less severe impact on the environment than wild fishing does. However, it's still important to make sure that whatever farmed fish you purchase was raised responsibly.

TIPS TO ELIMINATE FISHY SMELL

Fresh fish shouldn't have a very strong odor. It should smell like the sea water (or lake water) from which it was caught. If the fish is really fresh, it should give off a briny ocean smell. Sometimes, though, that "fishy" odor can turn you off from eating it.

So, what's with that fishy smell? According to the American Society for Nutrition, the smell associated with fish comes from their physiology. Fish use certain amino acids to help balance salt levels in their cells. When the fish are killed, bacteria and enzymes convert the amino acids to another compound that gives off that fishy odor.

You can reduce the odor in a few ways:

1. Make sure the fish is fresh. Rinse the fish with cold water to wash away any surface compounds, and treat the fish with an acidic ingredient such as lemon, vinegar, or tomato. Acid makes the bacteria and enzymes bind with water instead of with more of the amino acids, decreasing the odor.

2. Discard the packaging, and empty the garbage immediately after prepping the fish. This will keep the odor from spreading throughout your house.

3. Use the range hood or open a window to circulate fresh air.

4. After rinsing the fish, scrub your sink clean and sprinkle baking soda or sliced lemons down your garbage disposal. Again, acidic environments can prevent the odor-causing compounds from doing their thing.

One of the problems associated with aquaculture is potentially unsanitary and cramped enclosures for the fish, which can lead to the spread of disease among their populations. As a result, farmers often load up the fish with antibiotics, which can have adverse effects on the consumer.

As for wild-caught fish, their freshness is their greatest appeal, but the adverse environmental effects are a significant drawback. Overfishing of certain areas has caused whole populations of fish to swim farther out to sea, so the fishing boats follow and burn more and more fuel per trip, creating more and more pollution.

Both farm-raised and wild-caught fish have pros and cons, and it can be difficult to determine which fish and seafood to buy from which source. Thankfully, there are some wonderful organizations out there that want to help you make that decision. The best and most accessible resource is Seafood Watch, a program developed by the Monterey Bay Aquarium in California. Not only does the Seafood Watch website feature lists of sustainable fish, you can also get information on the risks and benefits of wild versus farm-raised fish, recommendations on which fish to purchase and which to avoid, and suggestions for good alternatives to the species of fish we should avoid. Seafood Watch is also available as an app on both iOS and Android platforms; the app helps folks choose restaurants and markets nationwide that offer ocean-friendly seafood.

THE SEAFOOD LOVER'S KITCHEN

Before setting off on a seafood-cooking adventure, it's important to prepare your kitchen. You can get a nice head start on things by stocking up on staple ingredients that appear in many of the recipes, as well as equipment that is essential to preparing them.

ESSENTIAL INGREDIENTS

Everyone needs a best friend in the kitchen—someone who's there for you when you need some extra support, the kind of friend who anticipates what you need and takes care of it before you even realize you needed the help. In this book, your best friend will be a well-stocked pantry, refrigerator, and freezer.

THE PANTRY

Begin stocking your pantry with the dry goods, canned, and spice staples that will be used frequently in the recipes to come:

Oils, vinegars, and sauces:

- cooking oil, vegetable
- olive oil, extra-virgin
- soy sauce
- Sriracha
- vinegar, red wine
- vinegar, white wine
- Worcestershire sauce

Cans and jars:

- beans
- broth, chicken and vegetable broth (for use in sauces)
- olives
- seafood, canned
- tomatoes, diced
- tomato paste
- tomato sauce

Spices and dried herbs:

- cayenne
- oregano
- paprika
- peppercorns, fresh (for grinding)
- red pepper flakes
- thyme
- salt, kosher

It's best to keep spices in a cool, dark cupboard away from your stovetop or other sources of heat. Whenever possible, buy the spices whole and grind them fresh as needed. Whole spices are more flavorful and last longer in cupboards than already-ground spices. Don't store your spices with baking flour and sugar; the baking ingredients can absorb the flavors and aromas of the spices over time.

Grains and starches:

- bread crumbs
- crackers (such as oyster crackers, for serving along-side soup)
- lentils
- pasta, dry (both long and short)
- rice, white and brown

THE REFRIGERATOR

Fresh fish can be stored in the refrigerator for one or two days before any unused portion will need to be frozen. Other ingredients to store in the refrigerator include:

- aromatics (like garlic, ginger, and fresh herbs)
- eggs
- produce
- proteins

THE FREEZER

Consider your freezer an essential part of your kitchen as well, particularly for storing fish that you're not quite ready to use or for leftovers.

- compound butters
- corn, frozen
- lobster (freeze the shells to make stock)
- peas, frozen
- shrimp
- stock, chicken and vegetable (if already opened)

ESSENTIAL EQUIPMENT

To cook fish at home successfully, you'll want to use good-quality tools. I encourage you to gather some well-made, high-quality items that you can rely on to make delicious food on your own.

CHEF KNIFE: Get the highest-quality chef knife that your budget allows. An 8-inch chef knife is the most commonly used size for home cooks, but the best one will be the one that feels the most comfortable in your hand. A sharp knife is a safe knife, so make sure to get your knives sharpened regularly.

TONGS: These are one of the few items for which I advise that buying cheaper is better, since they tend to wear out quickly. Tongs will be your extra hand in the kitchen.

WOODEN SPOONS: These are useful for stirring sauces, deglazing pans, and testing oil temperatures. Wood doesn't transfer heat as quickly as metal, so when you need to stir something over a hot stove, choose a wooden spoon.

FISH SPATULA: The unicorn of kitchen utensils! This spatula is thin and flexible, and its sharp edge slides underneath crispy pan-fried fish easily. It's long enough to balance the fish for easy flipping and is slightly angled so you can maneuver it in tight spaces.

DUTCH OVEN: Another multipurpose item, this can serve as a soup pot, braising pot, deep frying vessel and all around essential piece of cookware to keep on hand. Made from heavy cast iron, you can purchase varieties that are enamel coated which makes cleaning them a breeze. Because they are so dense and heavy, they hold their heat in well and can go from stovetop to oven to table easily.

SLOTTED SPOON: Like the fish spatula, the slotted spoon lifts just the food out of the pan allowing the liquid or oil to drip off and be used for a sauce.

FISH TWEEZERS: This is the best tool to pull out tiny bones in fish. They are angled for better positioning and can grip the bones tightly while you yank them out.

CAST IRON SKILLET: This is great for heartier fish, developing a crunchy crust, retaining heat, and having the ability to go from stovetop to oven.

SEAFOOD CRACKER AND CRAB PICKS: Seafood tools make it easier to open the shells and extract the delicate meat inside crab legs and claws. Some tool sets include small wooden mallets for cracking crab shells, making eating crab a lot of fun!

GUIDE TO SEAFOOD

There are two types of seafood: fish with fins, such as salmon and tuna, and shellfish, such as shrimp and clams. While they are both technically seafood, finfish and shellfish have significant biological distinctions.

FINFISH

Finfish, or simply "fish," have one central spine attached to a skull, breathe through gills, use fins to navigate through the water, and have protective scales covering their bodies. Finfish can fall into different groups based on their features.

DARK AND OIL RICH: anchovies, bluefin tuna, mackerel, wild Alaskan salmon, sardines

WHITE, LEAN, AND FIRM: catfish, haddock, Pacific cod, Pacific halibut, Pacific sole, striped bass, swordfish

MEDIUM COLOR AND OIL RICH: amberjack, Arctic char, Pacific Coho salmon, mahi-mahi, wahoo, yellowfin tuna

WHITE, LEAN, AND FLAKY: black sea bass, branzino, flounder, red snapper, tilapia, rainbow trout

WHITE, FIRM, AND OIL RICH: albacore tuna, Chilean sea bass, lake trout, lake whitefish, Pacific sablefish, white sturgeon

SHELLFISH

Shellfish fall into two groups: crustaceans and mollusks. Crustaceans are invertebrates with segmented bodies protected by hard shells that don't grow but periodically molt. They have eyes, and limbs that they use to move around. Mollusks are also invertebrates but do not have limbs or eyes and have even harder shells connected by a hinge to open and close. The exceptions are octopi and squid, which have both limbs and eyes but do not have hinged shells.

CRUSTACEANS: crab, lobster, crayfish, shrimp, and prawns

MOLLUSKS: clams, scallops, mussels, oysters, octopus, and squid

SHOPPING FOR SEAFOOD

If you are lucky enough to live in regions where fresh-caught fish (never frozen) is widely available, you've got it made. For most people, frozen fish is the best option because it's much more accessible. And sometimes canned fish is the way to go for simplicity's sake. When you're shopping for fresh fish, check for the following:

THE EYES: If the eyes look clear, wet, and shiny, the fish is most likely fresh. Cloudy or dry eyes can indicate old or improperly stored fish—definitely no longer fresh.

THE FINS: If the tail and side fins are full and intact, the fish is probably quite fresh; the fins will become dry and brittle when no longer fresh. Torn or ragged fins may indicate mishandling or improper storage.

THE FEEL: If you touch the fish, it should feel firm, wet, cold, and slippery (but not slimy). Press down, and the flesh should spring back. Pass on any fish that feels sticky, slimy, or soft.

THE GILLS: Pull back the gills on each side of the fish's head and have a look. The gills on fresh fish will be clean and red. If you see brown gills that look dark and slimy, the fish isn't fresh and is on its way to going bad.

THE SCALES: If you run your hands over the fish's scales, they should feel firm and look shiny. Dry, brittle scales indicate an old fish.

An important note about shopping for shrimp: In the US, shrimp are sized by how many there are in 1 pound. For example, "41–50," which generally refers to medium shrimp, means "41–50 shrimp per pound." It's more consistent than simply using small, medium, or large to designate size.

Depending on where you are, you may not have easy access to fresh, seasonal fish. In this case, frozen fish might be your best option for a couple of reasons. It is quite sustainable since it enables you to enjoy fish beyond its season and reduces food waste because frozen fish lasts longer in your freezer. It can be less expensive than fresh fish, especially in landlocked areas. And since fish can now be flash-frozen on the boat right after it's caught, all of its flavor, texture, and nutritional value are maintained. Make sure you never refreeze fish, though; once a fish has been defrosted it should be prepared as soon as possible. Some stores will display fish as if they're fresh, but the fish will actually be labeled "previously frozen." Make sure you look out for this designation and avoid refreezing previously frozen fish.

Another great way to enjoy fish is to make use of all the amazing canned (or tinned) fish available on the market. The fish is caught and quickly preserved, so it remains at its best as a shelf-stable product for much longer than even frozen fish. Canned fish is ready to eat and packed in oils that can improve the flavor of virtually anything you're preparing.

In fact, canned fish is perhaps the most sustainable of all. The fish used for canning is predominantly of the smaller type, such as sardines, skipjack tuna, and mackerel. Because they are shelf-stable, they need not be refrigerated, therefore using no energy except what was needed to process them before canning. The fish also doesn't spoil until the can is opened, eliminating unnecessary food waste. And here's a bonus: canned fish is also the least expensive on the market. When pressed for time, you can't go wrong with a delicious salad or pasta dish using canned fish.

TIPS FOR PURCHASING FROZEN SEAFOOD

Frozen fish is generally cheaper than fresh fish and can be used in many recipes without compromising flavor or texture. Look for the labels "Fresh Frozen" or "Flash Frozen"—they mean the fish was processed and frozen immediately after being caught, which preserves its texture, flavor, and nutritional value.

Also when checking labels, look for additives. Sodium tripolyphosphate is a chemical used to retain moisture. Although it's leached out during cooking, it adds weight to the frozen product which increases the price you pay for the fish.

If you come across frozen fish with lots of ice crystal buildup, do not buy it. It may have been stored improperly or mishandled. Specifically, stay away from fish that exhibits freezer burn—areas where the flesh is discolored or faded, or looks dried out.

A busy market generally means high turnover of their inventory, which means fresher seafood. Ask the person at the seafood counter how often their fish and seafood is restocked. Bring a cooler and an ice pack with you to take the fish home. Keeping the fish as cold as possible until you cook it will maintain its quality and freshness.

PREP AND STORAGE

Fresh fish can be expensive and is quite perishable, so it must be stored properly in the refrigerator until you're ready to use it. As soon as you get the fish home, follow these steps to keep your fish fresh. Using this method, fish will stay fresh for up to two days in the refrigerator. If you're using the fish immediately, simply complete steps 1 and 2.

1. Remove the fish from its packaging.

2. Rinse the fish under cold running water and blot dry with paper towels. Discard the paper towels immediately.

3. Place the fish on a rack in a single layer and avoid overlapping.

4. Set the rack with the fish inside a larger pan.

5. Cover the fish with crushed ice.

6. Cover the pan tightly with aluminum foil or plastic wrap and place it in the refrigerator. Check periodically and pour out water when the ice melts, replacing it with fresh ice. You do not want the fish resting in the ice water for too long.

If you don't plan to eat the fish within a couple of days after purchase, follow these steps to freeze it.

1. Wrap the fish tightly in plastic wrap and place the wrapped fish in a resealable bag, sealing tightly.

2. Label the bag with the type of fish and the date, and place it in the freezer for up to one month.

COOKING METHODS

Fish and seafood are versatile and can be cooked in a variety of ways that enhance their taste and texture, no matter what method you use. Here's an overview of the many ways to cook seafood.

PAN ROASTING: This is a two-step process. First you sear the fish over high heat in a pan or skillet, then you finish cooking it in the oven until done.

OVEN ROASTING: Oven roasting fish allows you to get a satisfying crunch without frying. Just because it's baked, though, doesn't mean it's healthy—watch the amount of butter or oil called for in the recipe. Oven roasting can also be the least "smelly" way to cook since the seafood is kept contained in the oven.

POACHING: Gently simmer the fish at a low temperature in a light stock such as chicken or vegetable stock until just cooked. This method is ideal for shrimp and other delicately textured seafood, and it keeps it moist.

SEARING: Cooking the fish in a pan or skillet over very high heat creates a deep, browned crust on the surface of the fish. Salmon, halibut, tuna, and other firm-textured fish are great for this method.

STEAMING: This is a quick and healthy way to cook any seafood without the use of any fat or oil.

GRILLING: Grilling fish is similar to searing in that it's done over high heat, but in this case you're using a ridged pan on the stove or a grate directly over a flame, creating dark char marks on the fish. This method is great for firm, textured fish that can withstand high heat.

BROILING: Broiling is a generally healthy cooking method that is fast, simple, and hassle-free, giving fish a nicely browned exterior. Just follow the basic grilling instructions above, and line the broiler pan with foil for easy cleanup.

DEEP FRYING: Submerging the fish in hot oil to cook is actually considered a dry-cooking method since water isn't being used. The resulting fish is crisp and crunchy on the outside and tender on the inside. A common misconception is that deep frying makes the food greasy, which is the case only if the oil temperature is not maintained.

Smoked Salmon with Baked Eggs
in Avocados, page 28

CHAPTER 2

BREAKFAST AND BRUNCH

SEAFOOD FOR BREAKFAST? YES, please! Because it's low in saturated fat but high in protein, fish and seafood are perfect for breakfast and won't leave you feeling sluggish or heavy like after a rich brunch. You can even prep your meal the night before, and when morning comes, you'll have an easy start to your day.

SMOI ED SALMON BENEDICT

NUT-FREE / 30 MINUTE / ONE POT
SERVES 4 / PREP TIME: 10 MINUTES / COOK TIME: 20 MINUTES

Smoked salmon and Eggs Benedict are two quintessential brunch items—so why not put them together? If you're short on time, serve the eggs sunny side up instead of poached.

FOR THE HOLLANDAISE SAUCE

3 cups water

1 egg yolk

2 tablespoons freshly squeezed lemon juice

⅛ teaspoon cayenne pepper

6 tablespoons unsalted butter, melted

Pinch kosher salt

FOR THE BENEDICT

4 eggs at room temperature

1 tablespoon white wine vinegar

2 English muffins split, toasted, and buttered

4 ounces smoked salmon or lox

1 tablespoon snipped chives (about 3 or 4 chive stalks)

TO MAKE THE HOLLANDAISE SAUCE

1. In a medium saucepan, bring the water to a simmer.

2. Find a glass mixing bowl wide enough to rest atop the saucepan and place it on the saucepan. Whisk in the egg yolk, lemon juice, and cayenne. Keep whisking until the yolk looks frothy and foamy, about 1 minute. Slowly drizzle in the melted butter while whisking vigorously until the sauce thickens and doubles in volume, about 3 minutes.

3. Season the sauce with the salt. Keep in a warm place until ready to use. Save the saucepan and simmering water for poaching the eggs.

TO MAKE THE BENEDICT

4. To poach the eggs, crack 1 egg into a small bowl. Add the vinegar to the simmering water. With a slotted spoon, stir the water quickly to create a whirlpool, and gently slip the egg into the vortex. Continue to gently swirl the water around the egg until the white just sets, about 15 seconds. Adjust the heat to make sure the water continues to simmer but not boil. Let the egg cook in the simmering water for another 3 minutes. With the slotted spoon, transfer the egg to a paper towel–lined plate. Repeat the process with the remaining eggs.

5. Assemble the Benedicts by placing each English muffin half on a warmed plate. Divide the smoked salmon and place on top of the muffins.

6. Place each poached egg on top of the smoked salmon and drizzle hollandaise sauce over each egg. Garnish with the chives and serve hot.

PRO TIP: Instead of hand whisking, use a handheld mixer or blender to make the hollandaise. Blend the yolk with the lemon juice and cayenne and then drizzle in the melted butter with the motor running. The sauce will have a beautiful velvety texture.

VARIATION TIP: Use crab cakes instead of smoked salmon for an extraordinary Crab Cake Benedict. Or use bagels in place of the English muffins for a winning combination of bagels and smoked salmon.

PER SERVING: Calories: 339; Total fat: 25g; Protein: 14g; Carbohydrates: 13g; Fiber: <1g; Sugar: 1g; Sodium: 768mg

SHRIMP OMELETS

GLUTEN-FREE / NUT-FREE / 5 INGREDIENT / 30 MINUTE / ONE POT
SERVES 4 / PREP TIME: 10 MINUTES / COOK TIME: 15 MINUTES

There are two types of omelets: folded and rolled. This recipe is written for the simple folded omelet, but don't let that keep you from trying the rolled version. These days, nonstick pans have superior performance that makes omelet cooking a breeze.

2 tablespoons extra-virgin olive oil

1 cup cooked bay shrimp

1 cup sliced scallions, white and green parts thinly sliced

Zest of 1 lemon (about 1 tablespoon)

Kosher salt

Freshly ground black pepper

8 tablespoons unsalted butter, divided

8 eggs, divided

1. In an 8-inch nonstick skillet, heat the olive oil over medium heat and stir in the shrimp and scallions. Gently sauté until just heated through. Transfer to a mixing bowl and stir in the lemon zest and a pinch each of salt and pepper. Set aside.

2. Wipe out the skillet and return it to medium heat. Add 2 tablespoons of butter and swirl to coat the pan as it melts. Crack 2 eggs into a bowl and whisk vigorously to beat the whites and yolks together. Season the eggs lightly with salt and pepper.

3. When the butter stops foaming, pour in the eggs and gently stir until the eggs just begin to set, about 2 minutes. Use a heatproof spatula to scrape the egg around the edges of the pan, carefully lifting and tilting the pan so that any runny egg runs underneath. Allow the eggs to cook for 45 seconds more, or until the surface of the eggs looks dry and matte (no runny eggs).

4. Add ¼ cup of the shrimp mixture to half of the eggs, then fold the other half over the top.

5. Slide the omelet onto a warmed plate. Repeat the process with the remaining butter, eggs, and shrimp. Garnish each omelet with any remaining filling.

PRO TIP: For a smoother omelet texture, blend the eggs in a blender. Measure the eggs in a liquid measuring cup and mix in enough water so that the eggs are at least 2 cups in volume. When making the omelets, use a ¼ cup measure for each.

SUBSTITUTION TIP: Use crabmeat or chopped lobster meat instead of shrimp. To garnish, chop some fresh tarragon instead of scallions. Or use smoked salmon instead of the shrimp, but do not add any additional salt, as the smoked salmon is salty enough.

PER SERVING: Calories: 386; Total fat: 28g; Protein: 30g; Carbohydrates: 3g; Fiber: 1g; Sugar: 1g; Sodium: 330mg

SMOKED MACKEREL KEDGEREE

GLUTEN-FREE / NUT-FREE / 30 MINUTE / ONE POT
SERVES 4 / PREP TIME: 10 MINUTES / COOK TIME: 20 MINUTES

Comfort food with a kick! This dish brings together flavorful spices and smoky mackerel with some bright spots of tomato, lemon zest, and cilantro. Kedgeree originates from India's *kitchari,* a lightly spiced rice and lentil dish. Smoked fish is flaked into the rice to make it a breakfast dish. It's a celebration of assertive flavors and the blending of cultures.

1 cup basmati rice

3 tablespoons unsalted butter

1 shallot, cut into ¼-inch cubes

Kosher salt

1 tablespoon curry powder

1 cup low-sodium chicken stock

1 can smoked mackerel, drained and flaked

2 Roma tomatoes, seeded and diced

Zest of 1 lemon

Juice of 1 lemon

Freshly ground black pepper

2 large eggs, hardboiled and sliced into 8 wedges each

2 tablespoons roughly chopped cilantro

1. In a large bowl, rinse the rice several times with cold water. When the water is no longer cloudy, cover the rice with cold water and soak for about 10 minutes.

2. While the rice is soaking, in a medium Dutch oven, melt the butter over medium heat and sauté the shallot with a pinch of salt for about 2 minutes, or until tender. Add the curry powder and sauté for a few seconds more, until the curry powder is fragrant.

3. Drain the rice into a sieve and add to the pan. Fry for about 1 minute, making sure the rice grains are coated with the butter and spices.

4. Add the chicken stock and another pinch of salt, and cover with the lid. Continue to cook for 2 minutes, then remove the pan from the heat and set aside for 10 minutes, still covered.

5. Remove the cover and add the mackerel, tomatoes, and lemon zest, gently folding the ingredients together. Season lightly with more salt and pepper. Transfer to a warmed serving platter and garnish with the sliced hardboiled eggs, cilantro, and a drizzle of lemon juice. Serve warm.

INGREDIENT TIP: Basmati rice is a long-grain rice that gets even longer as it cooks. Soaking the rice shortens the cooking time; however, to avoid soggy rice, it's important to fry it in step 3 before adding the cooking liquid.

SUBSTITUTION TIP: Add smoked sardines or hot smoked salmon to this dish. Make it even spicier by adding a pinch of chili powder to the spice mixture. If you're not into cilantro, replace it with a handful of chopped mint leaves for a burst of fresh flavor.

PER SERVING: Calories: 393; Total fat: 15g; Protein: 25g; Carbohydrates: 41g; Fiber: 2g; Sugar: 4g; Sodium: 267mg

HANGTOWN FRY

NUT-FREE / ONE POT
SERVES 4 TO 6 / PREP TIME: 15 MINUTES / COOK TIME: 25 MINUTES

During the California Gold Rush, the town of Placerville in the Sierra Foothills became known as "Hangtown," where the first uniquely Californian dish was developed. As the story goes, a Hangtown Fry became the most expensive dish served because of the ingredients: Oysters had to be brought in over ice from over 100 miles away in San Francisco, bacon was brought in via railroad from as far away as New York, and eggs were delicate and scarce. Miners who struck it rich would seek out this extravagant dish to celebrate. Here, I've simplified the dish by making it into an easy one-pan frittata.

4 strips bacon, diced

12 fresh oysters, shucked

Kosher salt

Freshly ground black pepper

¼ cup flour

8 eggs, divided

½ cup bread crumbs

2 tablespoons unsalted butter

2 scallions, white and green parts thinly sliced

1. In a 10- or 12-inch nonstick skillet, cook the bacon until brown and crispy, about 6 minutes. With a slotted spoon, remove the bacon and set on a paper towel–lined plate. Turn off the heat and keep the bacon fat in the pan.

2. Blot the oysters with a paper towel and season them on both sides with salt and pepper. In three separate bowls, place the flour, 1 beaten egg, and the bread crumbs.

3. Turn the heat back on to medium-high to reheat the bacon fat. One by one, coat the oysters with the flour, dip in the beaten egg, and then coat with the bread crumbs. Place the coated oysters in the pan. Cook the oysters until golden brown on both sides, 6 to 7 minutes in total, flipping them halfway through. Transfer to a paper towel–lined plate. Discard all but about 1 tablespoon of bacon fat from the pan and return the pan to the burner.

4. Whisk the remaining 7 eggs in a large bowl and season with salt and pepper. Melt the butter in the pan over medium-high heat, pour in the eggs, and stir gently until they just begin to set, 3 to 4 minutes. Sprinkle in the bacon and place the oysters around the pan. Cover and lower the heat to medium-low. Let the eggs continue to cook until the top is set, another 5 to 6 minutes.

5. Uncover the pan and sprinkle the scallions over the top. Loosen the edges of the frittata with a silicone spatula and carefully transfer to a warmed plate. Slice the frittata into wedges and serve hot.

SERVING TIP: For a more elegant presentation, serve a deconstructed Hangtown Fry. Place the fried oysters alongside some scrambled eggs and bacon, or pile them onto a slice of buttery brioche toast.

PER SERVING: Calories: 331; Total fat: 19g; Protein: 20g; Carbohydrates: 18g; Fiber: 1g; Sugar: 1g; Sodium: 375mg

CRAB STRATA WITH PIMENTOS AND CHEESE

NUT-FREE

SERVES 6 TO 8 / PREP TIME: 45 MINUTES / COOK TIME: 1 HOUR 10 MINUTES

Fret no more over what to serve for brunch—your go-to recipe is here! Serve your hungry guests this spectacularly effortless dish alongside a crisp salad.

3 tablespoons butter at room temperature, divided

½ medium yellow onion, cut into ¼-inch dice

1 (4-ounce) jar pimento strips, drained

2 tablespoons chopped fresh parsley

1 pound fresh lump crabmeat, picked through to remove the shells

1 loaf French bread, crusts trimmed and cut into 1-inch cubes (7 to 8 cups)

6 large eggs

2 cups half and half

Pinch kosher salt

⅛ teaspoon cayenne pepper

½ cup freshly grated Gruyère or Swiss cheese

1. Grease a 9-by-13-inch baking dish with 1 tablespoon of butter.

2. Melt the remaining 2 tablespoons of butter in a large nonstick skillet over medium-high heat and sauté the onion until soft, 4 to 6 minutes. Turn off the heat and stir in the pimentos and parsley.

3. Put the onion mixture in a mixing bowl and toss with the crab and bread cubes, then transfer to the greased baking dish.

4. In the same mixing bowl, whisk together the eggs, half and half, salt, and cayenne pepper. Pour the egg mixture over the crab and bread, and shake the dish gently to distribute the liquids. Let the mixture sit for 30 minutes, or covered and in the refrigerator over night.

5. Preheat the oven to 350°F.

6. Bake until golden brown and puffy, about 1 hour. Sprinkle the top of the strata with the cheese during the final 15 minutes of baking. Remove from the oven and cool on a wire rack for at least 30 minutes. The strata will deflate, which is normal.

7. Run a sharp paring knife around the edges to loosen the strata from the baking dish. Cut into 6 to 8 square pieces and serve hot.

VARIATION TIP: Change up the bread. Use buttery brioche or sourdough instead of French bread.

PREPARATION TIP: You can prepare the strata the night before. Cover tightly with plastic wrap or foil and refrigerate. The next morning slide it into the oven cold as it preheats (add about 20 minutes to the cook time if you do this).

PER SERVING: Calories: 579; Total fat: 34g; Protein: 23g; Carbohydrates: 45g; Fiber: 2g; Sugar: 4g; Sodium: 505mg

SALMON HASH WITH FRIED EGGS

GLUTEN-FREE / NUT-FREE / ONE POT
SERVES 4 / PREP TIME: 15 MINUTES / COOK TIME: 25 MINUTES

This light yet tasty dish is a great alternative to corned beef hash, as well as a great way to use up leftover salmon from a previous meal. When you have brunch at a restaurant, a dish like this is typically served with a poached egg, but I find a fried egg more appealing! You still get the runny yolk, but with crispy, lacy edges of the egg whites.

4 tablespoons unsalted butter

2 pounds Yukon Gold or red potatoes, scrubbed and boiled until just tender

1 large leek, rinsed well, trimmed, and thinly sliced crosswise

2 stalks celery, cut into ½ inch cubes

Kosher salt

Freshly ground black pepper

3 cups (6 ounces) cooked salmon, roughly flaked

2 tablespoons roughly chopped flat leaf parsley

4 eggs, fried, for serving

1. In a 12-inch cast iron skillet, melt the butter over medium heat and swirl to coat the pan. Lightly flatten the cooked potatoes on a cutting board or plate, and add them to the pan with the leek and celery. Gently break the potatoes into small, rough chunks, and sauté about 3 minutes. Season with salt and pepper and continue to sauté until the celery is tender, about another 3 minutes.

2. Increase the heat to medium-high and cook the potatoes until they brown slightly, 10 to 15 minutes. Add the salmon and parsley and cook just until the salmon is heated through. Use a flat silicone spatula to gently fold the salmon into the potatoes so the salmon doesn't break up too much. Add more salt and pepper to taste.

3. To serve, divide the salmon hash between warmed dinner plates and top each serving with a fried egg.

SUBSTITUTION TIP: Use smoked trout instead of cooked salmon.

COOKING TIP: Bake the eggs in the hash for an Instagram-worthy presentation! Use a large spoon to create 4 wells in the hash, then carefully crack the eggs into each well. Bake the hash in an oven preheated to 400°F for 6 to 8 minutes, or until the whites are set and the yolk is still runny. To serve, spoon the hash and egg together onto warmed plates.

PER SERVING: Calories: 407; Total fat: 19g; Protein: 19g; Carbohydrates: 40g; Fiber: 6g; Sugar: 3g; Sodium: 256mg

SMOKED TROUT AND BACON CORNMEAL WAFFLES

NUT-FREE / ONE POT

SERVES 4 / PREP TIME: 15 MINUTES / COOK TIME: 20 MINUTES

Savory waffles—yes, please! If you enjoy the sweet-savory balance, go ahead and serve maple syrup on these, but they are also fantastic topped with a fried egg and smothered with sour cream and herbs, like a tablespoon of chopped flat leaf parsley.

¾ cup all-purpose flour

¾ cup yellow cornmeal

1 teaspoon baking soda

1 teaspoon baking powder

½ teaspoon kosher salt

⅛ teaspoon cayenne pepper

1 cup buttermilk

1 large egg, separated

2 tablespoons unsalted butter, melted

8 ounces smoked trout, flaked

4 slices cooked bacon, finely chopped

½ cup sour cream

1. In a mixing bowl, stir together the flour, cornmeal, baking soda, baking powder, salt, and cayenne. Add the buttermilk, egg yolk, and butter, and mix until just combined. Fold in the trout and bacon.

2. In another bowl, vigorously whisk the egg whites until stiff peaks form, about 3 minutes. Gently fold the egg whites into the waffle batter until just combined.

3. Heat your waffle iron. Pour a scant 1 cup of the batter into the waffle iron and cook until golden brown on both sides. Repeat the process with the remaining batter.

4. Serve the waffles on warmed plates with a dollop of sour cream.

SUBSTITUTION TIP: Change things up and add 1 cup of chopped cooked shrimp or 1 cup of flaked canned salmon instead of the trout.

PER SERVING: Calories: 485; Total fat: 25g; Protein: 27g; Carbohydrates: 41g; Fiber: 2g; Sugar: 6g; Sodium: 1,684mg

SMOKED SALMON WITH BAKED EGGS IN AVOCADOS

NUT-FREE / 30 MINUTE / ONE POT
SERVES 4 / PREP TIME: 10 MINUTES / COOK TIME: 15 MINUTES

This decadent recipe ticks all the boxes for me—especially with a side of buttery toast! This dish makes for a great presentation; and if you nix the toast, it happens to be appropriate for those on a ketogenic diet. Garnish with minced chives for a pop of color.

2 extra-large avocados

Kosher salt

Freshly ground black pepper

2 ounces smoked salmon

4 large eggs

Pinch of red pepper flakes (optional)

1 tablespoon extra-virgin olive oil, for drizzling

4 slices sourdough bread, toasted

1. Preheat the oven to 400°F.

2. Cut the avocados in half and carefully remove the pits. Use a spoon to remove 1 or 2 scoops of the avocados' interiors to make larger cavities for the eggs. Reserve the scooped-out avocado for serving with the toast.

3. Place the avocados in an 8-by-8-inch baking dish. Season them with a pinch each of salt and pepper. Divide the smoked salmon slices evenly and place them into the avocados. Break the eggs carefully into the avocados over the salmon and season lightly with more salt and pepper. Sprinkle lightly with the red pepper flakes (if using).

4. Bake for 12 to 14 minutes, until the egg whites are set but the yolks are still runny.

5. Drizzle the tops of the eggs with the olive oil. Serve each avocado on a warmed plate with a slice of toast topped with the scooped-out avocado.

SERVING TIP: I like a splash of hot sauce over the eggs, but crumbled goat cheese is also a great flavor balance.

SUBSTITUTION TIP: Lump crabmeat (fresh or canned) goes great with avocado. Substitute ¼ cup of crabmeat for each slice of salmon.

PER SERVING: Calories: 400; Total fat: 25g; Protein: 15g; Carbohydrates: 31g; Fiber: 8g; Sugar: 3g; Sodium: 601mg

TUNA AND TOMATO FRITTATA

NUT-FREE / ONE POT
SERVES 4 TO 6 / PREP TIME: 10 MINUTES / COOK TIME: 25 MINUTES

Frittatas are a great way to fix a quick brunch for a crowd. You can use bits and pieces of leftover items from the refrigerator and mix them all with eggs. Some say a frittata is like crustless quiche, but for me it's more like an omelet. Serve a wedge of this frittata with a green salad or fruit, and your brunch is made!

1 tablespoon finely minced shallot

3 tablespoons extra-virgin olive oil

Kosher salt

Freshly ground black pepper

1 (6-ounce) can oil-packed tuna, drained

1 cup cooked bay shrimp

2 tablespoons unsalted butter

7 large eggs, beaten

1 cup grape tomatoes, halved

2 tablespoons roughly chopped flat leaf parsley

1. Preheat the oven to 400°F.

2. In a large nonstick skillet over medium heat, sauté the shallot in the olive oil and season lightly with salt and pepper. Sauté until the shallot is soft and translucent, about 3 minutes. Add the tuna and shrimp and sauté for 1 more minute, gently breaking the tuna into flakes.

3. Add the butter to the skillet, and when melted, pour in the eggs. Season lightly again with salt and pepper. Using a heatproof silicone spatula, gently move the eggs, tuna, and shrimp around the skillet until the eggs are just set but still runny, about 8 minutes.

4. Scatter the tomatoes over the eggs and slide the skillet into the oven. Bake for 10 minutes, or until the eggs are set and feel firm to the touch. Remove from the oven and cool for 5 minutes, then garnish with the parsley.

5. Run the spatula around the edges of the skillet and carefully slide the frittata onto a warmed plate. Slice the frittata into wedges and serve hot.

SUBSTITUTION TIP: Replace the tuna and shrimp with the same amount of chopped lobster for a spectacular twist on this brunch dish.

PER SERVING: Calories: 403; Total fat: 27g; Protein: 36g; Carbohydrates: 3g; Fiber: 1g; Sugar: 2g; Sodium: 456mg

CHILAQUILES WITH SAUTÉED SHRIMP

GLUTEN-FREE / NUT-FREE
SERVES 4 / PREP TIME: 15 MINUTES / COOK TIME: 20 MINUTES

Who can say no to crunchy tortilla chips tossed with a spicy sauce, tasty shrimp, and melty cheese? This traditional Mexican breakfast dish makes the most of leftover corn tortillas. This chips and salsa casserole is a comfort food that everyone will enjoy.

FOR THE SAUCE

2 cups of your favorite salsa

½ tablespoon chili powder

1 cup low-sodium chicken broth

Kosher salt

Freshly ground black pepper

FOR THE CHILAQUILES

2 tablespoons canola oil

1 pound medium shrimp (41–50 shrimp per pound), peeled and deveined

Kosher salt

Freshly ground black pepper

½ tablespoon chili powder

3 eggs, beaten

3 cups corn tortilla chips

½ cup shredded Jack cheese

½ cup sour cream

Sliced jalapeño pepper, for garnish (optional)

Chopped fresh cilantro, for garnish (optional)

TO MAKE THE SAUCE

1. Heat the salsa in a saucepan over medium-high heat with the chili powder. Stir in the chicken broth and bring to a boil. Season lightly with salt and pepper, and lower the heat to medium. Let the sauce simmer uncovered for 10 minutes. The liquid should reduce slightly.

TO MAKE THE CHILAQUILES

2. Preheat the oven to 400°F.

3. In a large cast iron skillet over medium heat, add the oil and swirl it around to coat the pan. When the oil is just beginning to smoke, add the shrimp, tipping the container away from you to avoid getting splashed by the hot oil. Season with salt and pepper and sauté until the shrimp turn pink and opaque, about 7 to 10 minutes. Stir in the chili powder.

4. Add the beaten eggs and scramble together with the shrimp. Then add ½ cup of the sauce and stir.

5. In a large mixing bowl, toss the tortilla chips with another 1 cup of the sauce. Add the chips to the skillet and toss gently with the shrimp and eggs. Sprinkle the cheese over the chips and slide the pan into the oven.

6. Bake for 10 minutes, or until the chips are heated through and the cheese has melted. Remove from the oven and top with the sour cream. Garnish with sliced jalapeños and cilantro (if using). Serve hot right from the pan.

SERVING TIP: The chips should be lightly coated with sauce, maintaining their bite. Soggy, mushy chips make for disappointing chilaquiles. Err on the side of undersaucing the chips and leave the remaining sauce to serve on the side.

COOKING TIP: If you don't have a large cast iron skillet, you can cook the shrimp and eggs in any pan you have, then toss together with the chips in a large mixing bowl. Transfer the chilaquiles to a casserole dish, top with the cheese, and bake.

PER SERVING: Calories: 472; Total fat: 24g; Protein: 40g; Carbohydrates: 26g; Fiber: 4g; Sugar: 8g; Sodium: 1,508mg

Clams Casino, page 48

CHAPTER 3

APPETIZERS AND SALADS

SERVING A SEAFOOD appetizer or salad can elevate a dinner party or a cozy dinner for two. In fact, every one of these dishes can be a great addition to a potluck party if you're asked to bring a dish. These are classic recipes you can depend on year after year.

CLASSIC CRAB CAKES

NUT-FREE / ONE POT
SERVES 4 / PREP TIME: 10 MINUTES, PLUS 1 HOUR TO CHILL / COOK TIME: 10 MINUTES

Crab cakes make a great appetizer for a dinner party, so use the best-quality crabmeat your budget allows. Chilling the cakes for at least 1 hour before cooking them is key: The time in the refrigerator helps bind the ingredients so they don't fall apart when you fry them. I like to serve these on top of a butter lettuce salad as a starter.

½ cup mayonnaise

1 large egg, beaten

1 teaspoon ground mustard

1 teaspoon Worcester-
shire sauce

1 teaspoon Old Bay seasoning

1 pound lump crabmeat

⅓ cup panko bread crumbs

2 tablespoons chopped fresh
flat-leaf parsley

Sea salt

Freshly ground black pepper

2 tablespoons vegetable oil

1 lemon, cut into 4 wedges,
for serving

1. In a medium mixing bowl, whisk together the mayonnaise, egg, mustard, Worcestershire sauce, and Old Bay seasoning. Add the crabmeat, bread crumbs, and parsley, and fold together gently. Season lightly with salt and pepper.

2. Divide the mixture into 4 equal portions and shape into cakes. Place the cakes on a plate and cover with plastic wrap. Refrigerate for at least 1 hour.

3. Heat the oil in a large nonstick skillet over medium-high heat until it begins to shimmer. Put the crab cakes in the skillet and cook for 6 to 7 minutes, flipping once when the underside is golden brown.

4. Transfer the crab cakes to 4 plates and season lightly with salt while they are still hot. Serve with the lemon wedges.

SUBSTITUTION TIP: You can make fish cakes with just about any cooked flaky fish such as salmon, tuna, or catfish.

INGREDIENT TIP: Plant-forward cooking is the way to a healthier planet and a healthier you. Add vegetables such as grated zucchini to the crab cakes; just squeeze as much moisture as possible from the grated zucchini before adding to the mixture.

PER SERVING: Calories: 537; Total fat: 46g; Protein: 12g; Carbohydrates: 20g; Fiber: 2g; Sugar: 4g; Sodium: 874mg

SHRIMP LOUIE

GLUTEN-FREE / NUT-FREE / 30 MINUTE / ONE POT
SERVES 4 / PREP TIME: 20 MINUTES / COOK TIME: 10 MINUTES

Shrimp Louie is a distinctly San Francisco dish, served mostly at seafood restaurants popular with tourists, but you don't have to go all the way to San Francisco to enjoy it.

FOR THE DRESSING

½ cup mayonnaise

1 tablespoon finely minced flat leaf parsley

2 tablespoons chili sauce (such as Heinz)

1 tablespoon ketchup

2 teaspoons freshly squeezed lemon juice

Kosher salt

Freshly ground black pepper

FOR THE SALAD

3 cups water

Kosher salt

1 tablespoon Old Bay Seasoning

½ pound medium shrimp (41–50 shrimp per pound), peeled and deveined

2 teaspoons freshly squeezed lemon juice

Freshly ground black pepper

1 head iceberg lettuce, torn into bite-size chunks

1 ripe avocado, cut into ½-inch cubes

1 cup grape tomatoes, halved

½ bunch asparagus, cut into bite-size pieces and blanched

2 hardboiled eggs, peeled and cut into 4 wedges each

TO MAKE THE DRESSING

1. In a small bowl, stir together the mayonnaise, parsley, chili sauce, ketchup, and lemon juice. Taste, and season with salt and pepper. Cover with plastic wrap and keep in the refrigerator until ready to use.

TO MAKE THE SALAD

2. In a saucepan over medium-high heat, add the water, a pinch of salt, and the Old Bay seasoning, and bring to a boil. Lower the heat to a simmer. Poach the shrimp in the simmering water for 6 to 8 minutes, or until the shrimp become pink and opaque.

3. Drain the water and transfer the shrimp to a small bowl. Drizzle with the lemon juice, cover, and refrigerate until ready to use.

4. On a chilled platter, arrange the lettuce and season lightly with salt and pepper. Assemble the salad starting with the shrimp in the center, and group the remaining components around the shrimp. Season again lightly with salt and pepper, then drizzle the dressing over the salad. Serve immediately.

SUBSTITUTION TIP: Shrimp Louie's fraternal twin, Crab Louie, can be made by replacing the shrimp with lump crabmeat and crab claws.

PER SERVING: Calories: 376; Total fat: 30g; Protein: 16g; Carbohydrates: 14g; Fiber: 6g; Sugar: 9g; Sodium: 902mg

SEARED AHI TUNA NIÇOISE SALAD

GLUTEN-FREE / NUT-FREE / ONE POT
SERVES 2 TO 4 / PREP TIME: 40 MINUTES / COOK TIME: 15 MINUTES

An intentionally composed salad celebrates a mixture of flavors, textures, and colors rather than being "tossed" all together in a heap. The individual components of this salad all require attention, but don't be intimidated by the work—the payoff is worth it. This one features a quickly seared, rare ahi tuna steak, but you can use oil-poached tuna or really any seafood in its place.

FOR THE VINAIGRETTE

1 tablespoon finely minced shallot (about half a medium shallot)

1 teaspoon whole-grain mustard

¼ cup white wine vinegar

1 teaspoon finely minced fresh thyme leaves

Pinch kosher salt

Pinch freshly ground black pepper

½ cup extra-virgin olive oil

FOR THE SALAD

1 (6-ounce) sushi-grade ahi tuna steak

Kosher salt

Freshly ground black pepper

2 tablespoons canola oil

Two handfuls salad greens

TO MAKE THE VINAIGRETTE

1. In a small bowl, whisk together the shallot, mustard, vinegar, thyme, salt, pepper, and olive oil. Set aside.

TO MAKE THE SALAD

2. Place the tuna on a cutting board and generously season both sides with salt and pepper.

3. Heat the oil in a cast iron skillet over high heat. Place the tuna in the pan and sear for 1 minute. Carefully flip the tuna and sear for another 45 seconds on the other side. Immediately plate the tuna and tent with foil for 10 minutes.

4. Lightly toss the salad greens with salt, pepper, and a splash of vinaigrette, and arrange on a serving platter.

5. Toss each salad component separately with about 1 teaspoon of vinaigrette, and place it on the salad platter, leaving room in the center for the tuna.

6. Slice the tuna across the grain into 8 slices and place in the center of the salad platter. Drizzle with any remaining vinaigrette and serve immediately.

- **4 small fingerling potatoes,** cooked and halved

- **12 green beans, blanched** and chilled

- **6 grape tomatoes, halved**

- **4 kalamata olives, pitted** and halved

- **1 small Persian cucumber,** halved lengthwise and cut into ½-inch chunks

- **2 hardboiled eggs, peeled and** quartered

SUBSTITUTION TIP: A grilled salmon fillet would make a fantastic substitute if tuna isn't available.

INGREDIENT TIP: If the very rare nature of the seared ahi isn't to your liking, you can serve a fully cooked tuna steak instead.

PER SERVING: Calories: 895; Total fat: 77g; Protein: 29g; Carbohydrates: 26g; Fiber: 5g; Sugar: 5g; Sodium: 341mg

CRAB POTSTICKERS

DAIRY-FREE / NUT-FREE / ONE POT
**SERVES 3 TO 4 / PREP TIME: 20 MINUTES, PLUS 50 MINUTES TO LET SIT AND TO CHILL /
COOK TIME: 20 MINUTES**

Potstickers are classic Chinese dumplings that are both steamed and pan-fried before serving. Nearly any dumpling with any filling can be cooked using this technique. You can easily prepare the dumplings in advance and freeze them. If you cook them from a frozen state, simply add 7 to 10 minutes to the steaming time.

1 cup napa cabbage, finely chopped

2 teaspoons kosher salt

½ pound lump crabmeat, picked through for shells and squeezed to remove moisture

1 teaspoon grated fresh ginger

1 scallion, finely diced

1 teaspoon soy sauce

1 teaspoon rice wine or cooking sherry

2 teaspoons sesame oil

12 fresh potsticker wrappers

2 tablespoons vegetable oil

½ cup water

1. In a large bowl, toss the napa cabbage with the salt and let sit for 30 minutes, or until the cabbage has wilted. Rinse the salt from the cabbage, then squeeze out as much water as possible. Return to the bowl.

2. Add the crabmeat, ginger, scallion, soy sauce, rice wine, and sesame oil, and mix together with the cabbage. Cover and refrigerate for at least 20 minutes, or up to 2 hours.

3. Line a baking sheet with parchment paper.

4. On a lightly floured surface, lay 1 potsticker wrapper. Place 1 scant tablespoon of crab filling in the center. Moisten the edges of the wrapper with a dab of water, then pleat one edge five times before pressing the edges together, creating a sealed pocket. Gently tap the potsticker on the board, creating a flat bottom with the pleats on top. Set the finished potsticker standing straight up on the prepared baking sheet. Repeat the process with the remaining wrappers and filling.

5. Heat the oil in a large nonstick skillet over medium-high heat. When the oil is almost smoking, arrange half the potstickers in the skillet as close to one another as possible without touching. Pan-fry for 2 to 3 minutes, checking frequently to make sure they're not burning. Reduce the heat if the bottoms are browning too quickly.

6. Carefully pour the water into the skillet. Cover, reduce the heat to low, and simmer for 8 to 10 minutes, or until most of the water has evaporated. Uncover, raise the heat back to medium-high, and cook for 2 to 3 minutes, or until all the water has evaporated and the bottoms of the potstickers are golden and crispy.

7. Transfer the potstickers to a serving plate and serve immediately.

PREPARATION TIP: Folding dumplings can be a challenge. If the pleating proves to be too tricky, fold up the edges to meet, and seal them tightly, making a half moon.

SUBSTITUTION TIP: If you can't find napa cabbage, substitute bok choy.

PER SERVING: Calories: 296; Total fat: 13g; Protein: 22g; Carbohydrates: 23g; Fiber: <1g; Sugar: <1g; Sodium: 2,123mg

LAYERED CALIFORNIA SUSHI DIP

GLUTEN-FREE / NUT-FREE
SERVES 6 TO 8 AS AN APPETIZER / PREP TIME: 15 MINUTES / COOK TIME: 25 MINUTES

This is a low-effort, high-impact dip your friends will be pleading for every time you throw a party! I borrowed this recipe from my sister-in-law and made a few minor adjustments to make it taste more like a California sushi roll. Furikake seasoning and dashi powder are sold in Asian markets and select grocery stores. If you can't find them, the dashi can be omitted; for the furikake, use 1 teaspoon each of toasted sesame seeds and chopped nori, plus a pinch each of salt and sugar.

Nonstick cooking spray

½ cup seasoned rice vinegar

2 tablespoons sugar

1 teaspoon powdered dashi

5 cups cooked rice

½ cup furikake seasoning

2 ripe avocados, pitted and thinly sliced

½ pound lump crabmeat, picked through for shells

¾ cup mayonnaise

¾ cup sour cream

8 to 12 snack-size packets of seasoned nori seaweed

1. Preheat the oven to 350°F. Spray a 9-by-13-inch baking dish with nonstick cooking spray and set aside.

2. In a small saucepan, heat the rice vinegar, sugar, and dashi over medium-low heat until it just begins to simmer and the sugar has dissolved, about 4 minutes.

3. Put the cooked rice in a mixing bowl. While the rice is still hot (heat it up if cold), drizzle the vinegar mixture over it and gently stir until well combined. Spread the rice in an even layer in the bottom of the baking dish, pressing down firmly to make a compacted bottom layer. Top the rice with half the furikake seasoning, then lay the avocado slices on top.

4. In the same bowl used for the rice, mix together the crabmeat, mayonnaise, and sour cream until combined. Spread the crab mixture evenly over the avocado.

5. Bake for 15 minutes, then switch the oven setting to broil. Broil for 5 to 6 minutes, or until the top looks golden and bubbly. Remove from the oven and sprinkle with the remaining furikake seasoning.

6. Cut the nori sheets in half. To serve, place a generous spoonful in a seasoned nori sheet and roll it up.

INGREDIENT TIP: Gild the lily by spreading a layer of tobiko, or flying fish roe, between the avocado and crab spread. The tiny caviar add a pleasantly crunchy texture to the dip.

PER SERVING: Calories: 717; Total fat: 38g; Protein: 18g; Carbohydrates: 64g; Fiber: 6g; Sugar: 15g; Sodium: 785mg

SHRIMP AND PAPAYA SALAD

GLUTEN-FREE / DAIRY-FREE / NUT-FREE / NO COOK
SERVES 4 / PREP TIME: 15 MINUTES, PLUS 30 MINUTES TO LET SIT

This tropical salad marries seafood and fruit in a startlingly delicious way. The creamy avocado blends the shrimp's brininess with the papaya's sweetness. The key to getting maximum flavor from this salad is to use the ripest papaya and avocado, and to let the salad rest before serving. The flavors bloom when the salad is served at room temperature.

2 ripe papayas, cut in half lengthwise, seeds removed

1 cup cooked medium shrimp (41–50 shrimp per pound), peeled and deveined and roughly chopped

1 avocado, peeled, pitted, and cut into ¼-inch cubes

1 medium red onion, diced

1 small jalapeño pepper, finely chopped

½ cup roughly chopped fresh cilantro

Zest of 2 limes

Juice of 2 limes

Kosher salt

Freshly ground black pepper

¼ cup extra-virgin olive oil

1. Use a spoon to scoop out the papaya, leaving about a ¼-inch layer of fruit in the skin. Cut the scooped out papaya into ¼-inch cubes and transfer to a mixing bowl.

2. Add the shrimp, avocado, onion, jalapeño, cilantro, lime zest, lime juice, and a pinch each of salt and pepper. Carefully toss the ingredients together so as not to mash up the avocado or papaya too much, then drizzle the olive oil over the top. Lightly season with salt and pepper to taste. Let the salad sit for 30 minutes to marry the flavors.

3. Spoon the salad into the halved papayas and serve immediately.

INGREDIENT TIP: Grilled shrimp tastes wonderful in this salad, so this is an especially great dish to make if you have leftover grilled shrimp from another recipe.

PREPARATION TIP: Refrigerate this salad for up to 30 minutes so that the flavors can marry and deepen, but be sure to let the salad come to room temperature before serving for the best taste.

PER SERVING: Calories: 347; Total fat: 22g; Protein: 20g; Carbohydrates: 22g; Fiber: 7g; Sugar: 14g; Sodium: 560mg

SALMON MOUSSE

GLUTEN-FREE / NUT-FREE / NO COOK
SERVES 10 TO 12 / PREP TIME: 20 MINUTES / CHILL TIME: 4 HOURS

In the 1980s, New York City's Upper West Side was home to the Silver Palate, an upscale gourmet deli and catering company. They created a salmon mousse that was raved over for decades. This is my variation on their recipe.

2 teaspoons vegetable oil, for lining the mold

1 (14½ ounce) can salmon, chilled

½ cup mayonnaise

½ cup Greek yogurt (any fat content you wish)

1 small shallot, chopped

2 teaspoons paprika

¼ teaspoon cayenne pepper

1 teaspoon kosher salt

2 tablespoons thinly sliced chives

2 teaspoons finely minced fresh dill

¼ ounce powdered gelatin (or 2½ teaspoons)

¼ cup cold water

2 tablespoons hot water

1 cup heavy cream, chilled

1. With your fingers or a piece of wax paper, rub a light layer of oil over the inside of a 5-cup serving bowl or decorative mold. Set aside.

2. In a food processor or blender, purée the salmon, mayonnaise, Greek yogurt, shallot, paprika, cayenne, and salt until smooth. Transfer to a mixing bowl and stir in the chives and dill.

3. In a small bowl, sprinkle the powdered gelatin over the cold water and wait until it blooms, about 5 minutes. Add the hot water and stir until the gelatin dissolves, then add to the salmon mixture and stir to combine.

4. Whip the heavy cream with a hand mixer until it forms stiff peaks. Gently fold the cream into the salmon mixture until just combined and transfer to your serving bowl or mold. Cover and refrigerate for up to 4 hours or overnight.

5. To serve, dip the bottom of the bowl or mold in a large pan of hot water to loosen the mousse. Put a plate on top of the mold and flip it over. Shake the mold gently to slide the mousse onto the plate and serve cold with crackers and crudités.

PREPARATION TIP: A chilled bowl, chilled beaters, and chilled heavy cream will whip the cream faster into stiff peaks.

SUBSTITUTION TIP: You can substitute leftover cooked salmon or smoked salmon in place of the canned salmon.

PER SERVING: Calories: 231; Total fat: 21g; Protein: 10g; Carbohydrates: 2g; Fiber: <1g; Sugar: 2g; Sodium: 336mg

CEVICHE

GLUTEN-FREE / DAIRY-FREE / NUT-FREE / NO COOK
SERVES 4 / PREP TIME: 10 MINUTES / CURE TIME: 1 HOUR

Ceviche originated in Peru but is widely enjoyed around the world. The citrus juices "cure" the fish without any heat. It's a great choice for a hot summer night when you can't bear to turn on the oven or the stove. Once, I served it in a chilled bowl surrounded with toasted tortilla chips for a party appetizer. "Great fishy salsa!" one guest exclaimed. Uh, thanks . . .

1 pound of sushi-grade whitefish (sole, snapper, halibut)

2 tablespoons diced red onion (⅛-inch cubes)

Juice of two limes

½ cup freshly squeezed lemon juice

½ cup freshly squeezed orange juice

1 generous pinch red pepper flakes

¼ cup olive oil

1 generous pinch kosher salt

2 tablespoons chopped cilantro

1. In a small mixing bowl, fold together the whitefish, onion, lime juice, lemon juice, orange juice, red pepper flakes, olive oil, and salt.

2. Cover and refrigerate for 1 hour; do not refrigerate for more than 2 hours or the fish will become tough.

3. Fold in the cilantro before serving.

SUBSTITUTION TIP: Any whitefish will do, but it needs to be of the highest quality, thus "sushi-grade," with bones and skin removed. Scallops and bay shrimp are delicious in ceviche too.

SERVING TIP: You can serve the ceviche with tortilla chips or endive spears, or in a bowl over a bed of Bibb lettuce. Top with minced serrano or jalapeño chile to add some heat.

PER SERVING: Calories: 307; Total fat: 17g; Protein: 31g; Carbohydrates: 6g; Fiber: <1g; Sugar: 4g; Sodium: 119mg

SHRIMP AND ORZO SALAD

DAIRY-FREE / NUT-FREE / ONE POT
SERVES 4 / PREP TIME: 15 MINUTES / COOK TIME: 15 MINUTES

This is an upscale version of pasta salad and makes for a terrific lunch or dish to take along to a picnic or potluck. Make it a day ahead and allow the flavors to combine so you have maximum deliciousness when you serve it.

1 pound jumbo shrimp (21–25 shrimp per pound), peeled and deveined

½ red onion, sliced into ¼-inch-wide strips (also known as a Lyonnaise cut)

2 garlic cloves, thinly sliced

2 cups grape tomatoes, halved

3 tablespoons extra-virgin olive oil, divided

Kosher salt

Freshly ground black pepper

Red pepper flakes

½ pound orzo pasta, cooked al dente

2 tablespoons roughly chopped fresh oregano

Zest of 1 lemon

Juice of 1 lemon

1. Preheat the oven to 400°F and line a sheet pan with foil or parchment paper.

2. Place the shrimp, onion, garlic, and tomatoes on the pan and toss with 2 tablespoons of olive oil. Season lightly with salt, pepper, and red pepper flakes.

3. Arrange the ingredients in a single layer on the pan and roast for 15 minutes, or until the tomatoes are blistered and the shrimp have turned pink and slightly opaque. Remove from the oven and tent with foil.

4. In a mixing bowl, toss together the orzo, the oregano, the remaining 1 tablespoon of olive oil, the lemon zest, and the lemon juice. Add the shrimp, onion, garlic, and tomatoes, and stir to combine. Divide among 4 plates and enjoy immediately.

COOKING TIP: Skewer the shrimp, onion, and tomatoes, and grill instead of roasting to give the salad a slightly charred, smoky flavor.

SERVING TIP: Garnish the salad with ¼ cup of crumbled feta cheese.

PER SERVING: Calories: 451; Total fat: 15g; Protein: 37g; Carbohydrates: 49g; Fiber: 4g; Sugar: 5g; Sodium: 347mg

CRAB RANGOONS

NUT-FREE / 30 MINUTE / ONE POT
SERVES 4 AS AN APPETIZER / PREP TIME: 15 MINUTES / COOK TIME: 8 TO 10 MINUTES

These deep-fried crab dumplings first appeared on the scene in 1956 at Trader Vic's, a popular Polynesian-style restaurant in San Francisco. In the late 1980s at San Francisco State University where I went to school, there was a Chinese takeout counter in the basement of the student union. I would buy these and bring them to my afternoon class every day to eat for lunch.

4 ounces cream cheese, softened

4 ounces (¼ pound) fresh lump crabmeat, picked through for shells and squeezed to remove moisture

1 green onion, finely minced

2 garlic cloves, finely minced

2 teaspoons curry powder

½ teaspoon Worcestershire sauce

1 teaspoon kosher salt, divided

12 fresh wonton wrappers

1 large egg, beaten

3 cups canola oil

1. In a small mixing bowl, mix together the cream cheese, crabmeat, green onion, garlic, curry powder, and Worcestershire sauce until just combined. Season lightly with salt if needed.

2. Lay one wonton wrapper on a clean work surface. Place 1 teaspoon of the crab filling in the middle of the wrapper. With your fingertip or a pastry brush, lightly brush the edges of the wrapper with the egg wash. Bring the opposite corners of the wrapper to touch and seal the seams to make an X. Repeat with the remaining wonton wrappers and filling.

3. Pour the oil into a Dutch oven and heat to 375°F over medium heat. You can tell the oil is at the right temperature when it bubbles around a piece of bread or the end of a wooden spoon when dipped in. Working in batches, place 3 or 4 rangoons in the hot oil and cook until golden and crispy, about 4 to 5 minutes. Using a wire skimmer, transfer the rangoons to a wire rack to cool and drain the excess oil. Lightly sprinkle the rangoons with salt and serve immediately.

INGREDIENT TIP: Canned crab will work just as well as fresh crab in this recipe.

COOKING TIP: For a slightly healthier version, brush the dumplings with a little melted butter and bake for 15 minutes at 425°F.

PER SERVING: Calories: 707; Total fat: 66g; Protein: 13g; Carbohydrates: 17g; Fiber: 1g; Sugar: 1g; Sodium: 936mg

CLAMS CASINO

NUT-FREE

SERVES 4 AS AN APPETIZER / PREP TIME: 20 MINUTES / COOK TIME: 25 MINUTES

Though this recipe originated in Rhode Island, you can find it on nearly every menu in New York City's Little Italy. They make great little appetizers for a dinner party and can be prepared ahead of time and popped into the oven just before the guests arrive.

12 littleneck clams, scrubbed well under cold water

¼ cup water

4 slices bacon, cut widthwise into ¼-inch strips

1 tablespoon unsalted butter

1 (4 ounce) jar diced pimentos, drained

1 small shallot, finely minced

2 garlic cloves, finely minced

Kosher salt

Freshly ground black pepper

1 tablespoon roughly chopped fresh oregano leaves

¾ cup panko bread crumbs

1 tablespoon minced flat leaf parsley

1 tablespoon grated Parmesan cheese

1 lemon, cut into wedges

1. Add the clams to a medium saucepan and pour the water over them. Turn the heat to medium-high and put the lid on. Steam the clams for 6 to 7 minutes, or until they've all completely opened. Remove the pan from the heat and set aside to cool slightly.

2. Set a bowl on the counter to catch any juice that runs out of the clams as you shell them. When the clams are cool enough to handle, remove the top shell (the deeper shell is the bottom one) of each clam and run a spoon under the clam to dislodge it from the shell and turn it over (this will make it much easier to spear with a fork and eat). Arrange the clams in their bottom shells in a single layer in a 9-by-13-inch baking dish. Strain the clam juice and set it aside.

3. In a nonstick pan over medium-high heat, cook the bacon until just brown but not yet crisp, about 5 to 6 minutes. Transfer the bacon with a slotted spoon to a paper towel–lined plate and set aside. Discard the bacon fat, but do not discard the lovely brown buildup from the bacon clinging to the pan.

4. Return the pan to medium-high heat and melt the butter. Sauté the pimentos, shallot, and garlic for about 4 minutes. Season lightly with salt and pepper and add 2 tablespoons of the reserved clam juice to deglaze the pan. Continue cooking until the clam juice has evaporated, about 2 more minutes. Turn off the heat and set the pan aside to cool.

5. Set the broiler on high.

6. Return the pan to your work surface and stir in the oregano, bread crumbs, parsley, and cheese. Divide this mixture over each clam. Top with the bacon strips.

7. Broil the dish for 3 to 5 minutes, or until the bacon is crispy and the bread crumbs are toasted and golden. Squeeze the lemon over the clams and serve immediately.

SUBSTITUTION TIP: Using mussels instead of clams turns this dish into moules gratinée. Mussels are much smaller than littleneck clams, so be sure to prepare twice as many mussels, and cook them for half the time.

PER SERVING: Calories: 182; Total fat: 7g; Protein: 11g; Carbohydrates: 21g; Fiber: 3g; Sugar: 2g; Sodium: 243mg

SMOKED TROUT AND APPLE SALAD

GLUTEN-FREE / NUT-FREE / 30 MINUTE / NO COOK
SERVES 4 / PREP TIME: 10 MINUTES

Salads served as a first course are intended to whet the appetite so the diner "anticipates" what's coming next as the entrée. Conversely, salads served as the last course of the meal are intended to cleanse the palate, to cut through the rich meal, and to aid in digestion. This Smoked Trout and Apple Salad could stand in for either course. The smoky, buttery trout pairs beautifully with the tart apple and tangy buttermilk dressing.

FOR THE DRESSING

¼ cup mayonnaise

2 tablespoons buttermilk

1 tablespoon prepared horseradish, drained

2 tablespoons chives, finely minced

2 tablespoons extra-virgin olive oil

Kosher salt

Freshly ground black pepper

FOR THE SALAD

5 ounces spring mix salad greens

1 large Granny Smith apple, thinly sliced and cut into matchsticks

5 ounces smoked trout, boned, skinned, and flesh flaked

TO MAKE THE DRESSING

1. In a small bowl, whisk together the mayonnaise, buttermilk, horseradish, chives, and olive oil. Lightly season with salt and pepper and set aside.

TO MAKE THE SALAD

2. In a large mixing bowl, toss the spring mix and apple together with half the dressing, and divide equally among 4 chilled salad plates.

3. Toss the trout in the same bowl with half the remaining dressing. Divide the trout among the salad plates, drizzle the remaining dressing over the top, and serve immediately.

PREPARATION TIP: Make the dressing ahead of time in order to save time.

PER SERVING: Calories: 248; Total fat: 20g; Protein: 9g; Carbohydrates: 10g; Fiber: 2g; Sugar: 8g; Sodium: 396mg

SMOKED SALMON DEVILED EGGS

GLUTEN-FREE / NUT-FREE / 30 MINUTE
SERVES 4 AS AN APPETIZER / PREP TIME: 15 MINUTES

Deviled eggs are an appropriate hors d'oeuvre to serve for any occasion. Adding smoked salmon to the deviled yolks gives this dish an extra layer of decadence, not to mention extra protein. Reserve 1 tablespoon of the filling and smear a dab on the platter to anchor each of the eggs; this will keep them from sliding around on the platter.

6 large eggs, hardboiled, then peeled

½ cup finely diced smoked salmon

2 tablespoons thinly sliced fresh chives, divided

2 tablespoons plain Greek yogurt (any fat content)

2 teaspoons finely minced shallot

1 teaspoon capers, rinsed and finely minced

Zest of ½ lemon

1 teaspoon freshly squeezed lemon juice

1 tablespoon extra-virgin olive oil

1. Peel the eggs and halve them lengthwise. Remove the yolks and in a small mixing bowl mash them with a fork until crumbled.

2. Add the salmon, 1 tablespoon of chives, the yogurt, the shallot, the capers, the lemon zest, and the lemon juice. Mix until all the ingredients are combined.

3. Scoop the yolk mixture back into the cavities of the egg whites and arrange on a platter. Sprinkle the remaining 1 tablespoon of chives over the eggs and drizzle with the olive oil. Serve immediately.

SUBSTITUTION TIP: Try finely chopped crabmeat or shrimp instead of the salmon.

PER SERVING: Calories: 162; Total fat: 12g; Protein: 13g; Carbohydrates: 1g; Fiber: <1g; Sugar: 1g; Sodium: 416mg

CHINESE SHRIMP TOAST

NUT-FREE / ONE POT
**SERVES 4 TO 6 AS AN APPETIZER / PREP TIME: 35 MINUTES, PLUS 30 MINUTES TO CHILL /
COOK TIME: 15 MINUTES**

As the story goes, this dish originally came about to make use of leftover shrimp dumpling filling in a Chinese restaurant. A cook spread the filling on a piece of bread and fried it—thus beginning the tradition of shrimp toast. These savory, crunchy snacks could be the thing to replace wings or nachos at your next party. Make a lot of them, though, because they will be gone in a flash!

**¾ pound raw shrimp, peeled
and deveined**

**3 tablespoons roughly
chopped water chestnuts**

4 scallions, roughly chopped

**3 garlic cloves,
roughly chopped**

**1-inch piece fresh ginger,
roughly chopped**

**2 teaspoons toasted
sesame oil**

2 teaspoons fish sauce

1 tablespoon soy sauce

1 large egg white

**¼ teaspoon ground
white pepper**

**4 large slices white sandwich
bread, lightly toasted and
crusts trimmed**

**1 to 1½ cups vegetable oil,
for frying**

Pinch kosher salt

**2 teaspoons toasted
sesame seeds**

**2 tablespoons chopped fresh
cilantro (optional)**

1. Put the shrimp, water chestnuts, scallions, garlic, ginger, sesame oil, fish sauce, soy sauce, egg white, and white pepper in the bowl of a food processor. Pulse several times, then scrape down the sides of the bowl, and continue to process until the mixture is well blended and resembles a paste. Transfer the mixture to a bowl and cover with plastic wrap. Chill in the refrigerator for up to 30 minutes.

2. Spread an even layer of the shrimp paste on each of the toasts, matching the thickness of the spread paste to that of the bread and making sure to spread right to the edges of the toast. Cut the toasts in half diagonally and again cut each toast triangle in half diagonally.

3. Pour enough vegetable oil into a nonstick skillet to cover the bottom by half an inch. Turn the heat to medium-high and check the temperature by dipping a piece of the trimmed crust into the oil. If the oil begins to bubble and boil around the crust, the oil is at the right temperature for frying.

4. Working in batches, place the toasts paste-side down in the oil in a single layer without overlapping, being careful to lower them into the oil away from you to avoid splashing. Fry the toasts until the paste turns golden brown and crispy, about 3 minutes, then flip and fry the other side for about 3 minutes. Transfer the toasts to a paper towel–lined plate to drain the excess oil, and season the toasts with the salt while they're still hot. Repeat the process with the remaining toasts.

5. Transfer the toasts to a warmed platter and top with the sesame seeds. Garnish with the cilantro (if using). Serve immediately.

PREPARATION TIP: If you don't have a food processor, chop each solid shrimp paste ingredient as finely as possible, then pile them all together and mince on a cutting board until the mixture resembles a paste. Transfer the paste to a mixing bowl and stir in the liquid ingredients.

SUBSTITUTION TIP: Switch out the shrimp and use cooked crab or raw salmon instead.

PER SERVING: Calories: 481; Total fat: 33g; Protein: 21g; Carbohydrates: 26g; Fiber: 1g; Sugar: 4g; Sodium: 806mg

SUMMER ROLLS

GLUTEN-FREE / DAIRY-FREE / NUT-FREE / 30 MINUTES / NO COOK
SERVES 4 / PREP TIME: 25 MINUTES

One of the first restaurant jobs I had was in a seafood restaurant, where I shucked oysters and made sushi rolls and summer rolls. I've realized since then that summer rolls can be filled with just about any combination of protein, herbs, and vegetables as long as there is a balance of cooked and raw, sweet and sour, and hot and cold.

FOR THE DIPPING SAUCE

1 tablespoon fish sauce

2 teaspoons sugar, or to taste

2 teaspoons freshly squeezed lime juice

1 teaspoon grated fresh ginger

1 small Thai bird chile, roughly chopped (optional)

1 teaspoon water, if needed

FOR THE ROLLS

12 (8-inch) rice paper rounds

6 red leaf lettuce leaves, washed and shredded

½ pound cooked rice vermicelli, drained and rinsed

½ cup shredded carrots

½ cup fresh mint leaves

½ cup fresh Thai basil leaves

12 large cooked shrimp (31–35), halved lengthwise

TO MAKE THE DIPPING SAUCE

1. In a small bowl, stir together the fish sauce, sugar, lime juice, ginger, and Thai bird chile (if using). Taste, and add the water to thin out the sauce if needed.

TO MAKE THE ROLLS

2. Pour 2 cups of warm water into a pie plate or shallow baking dish and dip the rice paper in the water one sheet at a time, then lay the sheets on a cutting board. Wait a few seconds for the rice paper to soften and become pliable.

3. Place a bit of lettuce, rice vermicelli, carrot, mint, Thai basil, and shrimp on the bottom third of the rice paper. Fold the bottom edge over the ingredients, then fold in the sides. Roll away from you into a tight, compact little tube. Set aside on a serving platter and repeat until you have 12 rolls.

4. To serve, slice each roll in half and arrange on a platter with the dipping sauce on the side.

SERVING TIP: Serve the summer rolls immediately, or cover and set aside for up to 2 hours. Do not refrigerate, or the rice paper will become hard.

PER SERVING: Calories: 175; Total fat: 1g; Protein: 14g; Carbohydrates: 38g; Fiber: 1g; Sugar: 4g; Sodium: 700mg

Spicy Thai Coconut Shrimp Soup, page 68

SOUPS AND SANDWICHES

YOU CAN NEVER go wrong serving seafood for lunch or a light supper. Satisfying soups and hearty sandwiches keep your cooking repertoire interesting and varied. A nice thing about adding seafood to soups and sandwiches is that you can save time by using leftovers from a previous dinner to add into your dishes.

QUICK AND EASY OYSTER PO' BOYS

NUT-FREE
SERVES 2 TO 4 / PREP TIME: 15 MINUTES / COOK TIME: 20 MINUTES

This recipe covers all the bases for a classic fried oyster po' boy, but is simplified, without the fuss of deep-frying. You still get the flavor and texture profiles but with much less time and effort. If good quality oysters aren't available, consider swapping for shrimp or a slab of catfish instead.

FOR THE OYSTERS

3 tablespoons vegetable oil

6 to 8 fresh oysters, shucked

Kosher salt

Freshly ground black pepper

2 cups all-purpose flour, plus more if needed

1 large egg, beaten

2 cups panko bread crumbs

FOR THE SANDWICH

3 tablespoons mayonnaise

2 teaspoons prepared horseradish

1 teaspoon Creole seasoning

1 teaspoon freshly squeezed lemon juice

Kosher salt

Freshly ground pepper

2 French sandwich rolls, split in half

2 or 3 leaves green leaf lettuce, washed and spun dry

2 ripe Roma tomatoes, cut into ¼-inch-thick slices

TO MAKE THE OYSTERS

1. In a large nonstick skillet, heat the oil over medium-high heat. While the pan is heating, blot the oysters with a paper towel and season both sides with salt and pepper. Put the flour, beaten egg, and bread crumbs in three separate bowls or shallow dishes.

2. Take one oyster and coat it with flour, dip it in the beaten egg, and coat it with bread crumbs. Repeat with the remaining oysters, then place them in the pan, working in batches so as not to crowd the pan. Fry the oysters until golden brown on both sides, flipping them halfway through, about 6 to 7 minutes in total. Transfer to a paper towel–lined plate.

TO ASSEMBLE THE SANDWICH

3. Set the broiler to high. Line a baking sheet with foil and set aside.

4. In a small bowl, mix together the mayonnaise, horseradish, Creole seasoning, and lemon juice, and season with salt and pepper.

5. Toast the bread slightly by broiling it for a few seconds until it turns lightly toasty. Transfer the rolls to warmed plates and spread the mayonnaise mixture on one side of each roll. Evenly divide the oysters among the rolls and top with the sliced tomatoes and lettuce. Serve hot.

INGREDIENT TIP: If you don't want to bother with shucking the oysters for this sandwich, fresh oysters from a jar will do just fine. You can find these at the supermarket seafood counter.

PER SERVING: Calories: 1,378; Total fat: 43g; Protein: 35g; Carbohydrates: 214g; Fiber: 10g; Sugar: 14g; Sodium: 1,450mg

NEW ENGLAND CLAM CHOWDER

NUT-FREE
SERVES 4 TO 6 / PREP TIME: 15 MINUTES / COOK TIME: 35 MINUTES

Also known as Boston chowder or white clam chowder, this version is more popular than its cousin, red or Manhattan clam chowder. It's typical in San Francisco to serve the chowder in hollowed-out sourdough bread bowls—you get to eat the vessel in which the soup is served! The Pier Chowder House in Point Arena, California, actually takes the interior part of the bread, and fries it to make chunky croutons to serve with the soup. This is a simpler but no less delicious version, served in regular bowls.

2 large russet potatoes, peeled and cut into ½-inch cubes

Generous pinch kosher salt, plus more if needed

2 tablespoons unsalted butter

3 slices bacon, finely chopped

1 large yellow onion, cut into ¼-inch cubes

2 large celery stalks, cut into ¼-inch cubes

2 garlic cloves, finely minced

1 bay leaf

3 tablespoons all-purpose flour

4 cups whole milk

4 (6½-ounce) cans chopped clams

3 or 4 dashes Tabasco sauce

Chopped fresh parsley, for garnish (optional)

1. In a large saucepan, cover the potatoes with cold water and add the salt. Bring to a boil over high heat. Reduce the heat to medium-low, cover, and simmer until the potatoes are tender, about 10 to 12 minutes. Remove from the heat and drain, reserving 2 cups of the cooking water.

2. In a Dutch oven, melt the butter over medium heat. Add the bacon and cook until it begins to brown, about 6 minutes. Add the onion, celery, garlic, and bay leaf. Sauté until the vegetables soften, about 5 to 6 minutes.

3. Sprinkle the flour over the vegetables and stir to coat, cooking for 2 minutes (do not allow the flour to brown). Gradually whisk in the milk and add the potatoes, clams (with juices), and Tabasco sauce.

4. Simmer the chowder for 10 minutes, stirring frequently. Taste and add salt if needed. If the chowder becomes too thick, adjust the texture by adding ¼ cup at a time of the reserved potato liquid. Discard the bay leaf and serve in warmed soup bowls, garnished with chopped parsley (if using).

VARIATION TIP: Morph this into a corn and shrimp chowder by using 1 cup of fish stock instead of the clam juice, and stirring in 1 cup of frozen corn kernels and 1 cup of chopped cooked shrimp.

SERVING TIP: The classic accompaniments to this soup are saltines or oyster crackers. The crackers can be crushed and added to help thicken the soup's texture, as traditional New England clam chowder is actually thinner than most people expect.

PER SERVING: Calories: 507; Total fat: 16g; Protein: 29g; Carbohydrates: 61g; Fiber: 4g; Sugar: 14g; Sodium: 1,440mg

CRAB BISQUE

NUT-FREE
SERVES 4 / PREP TIME: 40 MINUTES / COOK TIME: 1 HOUR

Creamy and velvety, this luxuriously decadent soup is perfect for special occasions and holidays. Traditional methods for making bisque include grinding the crab shells to a paste and using it to thicken the soup. Here, we roast the shells to make a flavorful stock and use rice to thicken the soup instead.

FOR THE STOCK

2 large cooked Dungeness crabs, shells intact

2 tablespoons tomato paste

2 tablespoons vegetable oil

2 quarts low-sodium vegetable broth

1 bay leaf

FOR THE BISQUE

2 tablespoons unsalted butter

1 shallot, finely chopped

1 carrot, finely chopped

2 tablespoons tomato paste

Pinch of cayenne pepper

¾ cup dry white wine

1 quart crab broth

¼ cup white rice

Kosher salt

1 cup heavy cream

TO MAKE THE STOCK

1. Preheat the oven to 400°F.

2. Crack the crab shells with seafood crackers or sharp shears and pick out the meat. Set the crabmeat aside. Toss the crab shells, tomato paste, and vegetable oil together in a roasting pan and roast for 10 to 12 minutes.

3. Transfer the shells to a stockpot and cover with vegetable broth by 2 inches. Add the bay leaf and heat over medium-high heat until the stock starts to simmer, then lower the heat to medium-low. Keep it at a low simmer for 40 minutes, skimming off the foam as it forms on the surface. Do not stir or disturb the stock as it simmers—that will result in a cloudy stock. This will become the base for your crab bisque.

TO MAKE THE BISQUE

4. While the stock is simmering, melt the butter in a Dutch oven over medium-high heat and sauté the shallot and carrot until soft, about 7 minutes. Add the tomato paste and cayenne pepper, sautéing to deepen the color and flavor of the tomato paste, about 3 minutes.

5. Add the wine to deglaze the pan, dissolving any buildup stuck to the pan. Reduce the wine until nearly evaporated, 4 to 5 minutes.

6. After the stock has finished simmering, strain and discard the solids, then add the stock and the uncooked rice to the Dutch oven and increase the heat to medium-high. Simmer for 20 minutes, or until the rice is fully cooked.

7. Turn off the heat. Reserve ½ cup of the crabmeat and stir the rest into the soup. Let the soup cool for a few minutes before blending. If using a blender, make sure the soup is cool enough to blend, or use an immersion blender directly in the pot. Blend until the soup is smooth and all the solids are completely puréed. If the purée is too thick, add more stock a small bit at a time. The consistency is right when the soup coats the back of a spoon. Taste, and season with salt.

8. Return the puréed soup to the pot (unless it was blended directly in the pot), and stir in the cream and remaining crabmeat. Divide the soup among warmed soup bowls and serve hot.

INGREDIENT TIP: Save yourself some time and buy the crabs already cooked from the seafood counter—just make sure the shells are intact so you can make the stock. If you like, you can make the stock ahead of time and freeze both the stock and the crabmeat until you're ready to make the soup.

SUBSTITUTION TIP: You can also make bisque from other shellfish like shrimp or lobster. If you're going to use lobster for soup making, save some bucks by opting for frozen over fresh.

PER SERVING: Calories: 540; Total fat: 36g; Protein: 17g; Carbohydrates: 22g; Fiber: 1g; Sugar: 8g; Sodium: 1,277mg

CLASSIC CREOLE SHRIMP GUMBO

DAIRY-FREE / NUT-FREE / ONE POT
SERVES 6 TO 8 / PREP TIME: 15 MINUTES / COOK TIME: 40 MINUTES

Achieving authentic flavors in gumbo is as easy as knowing which ingredients to use and having the patience to cook the roux to its dark brown color. The combination of onion, celery, and green bell pepper, known as the "holy trinity," as well as the chocolate-brown roux give this stew its characteristic flavor.

3 tablespoons vegetable oil

3 tablespoons unbleached all-purpose flour

1 yellow onion, cut into ¼-inch cubes

2 celery stalks, cut into ¼-inch cubes

1 green bell pepper, cut into ¼-inch cubes

¼ teaspoon cayenne pepper

Kosher salt

Freshly ground black pepper

1 bay leaf

2 teaspoons dried thyme

4 garlic cloves, finely minced

4 cups low-sodium chicken broth

1 pound raw medium shrimp (41–50 shrimp per pound), peeled and deveined

1 cup frozen chopped okra

Sliced scallions, for garnish (optional)

1. In a large Dutch oven over medium heat, add the oil and flour. Whisk together until smooth, then use a wooden spoon or silicone spatula to stir occasionally. Cook the roux until it turns a deep brown color, almost like milk chocolate, about 15 to 20 minutes. Adjust the heat to keep the roux from burning.

2. Quickly add the onion, celery, and bell pepper to keep the roux from burning, and cook until tender, 7 to 8 minutes. Add the cayenne pepper and season with salt and pepper. Add the bay leaf, thyme, and garlic, and stir to combine. Sauté for about 1 minute more, or until the garlic becomes fragrant.

3. Add the chicken broth, increase the heat to medium-high, and bring to a simmer, stirring frequently until the broth thickens slightly. Add the shrimp and okra and turn the heat back down to medium. Simmer for 8 to 10 minutes more, or until the shrimp is pink and opaque and the okra is tender.

4. Remove the bay leaf. Taste and season with salt and pepper again if needed. To serve, divide the gumbo into warmed soup bowls. Scallions are an optional garnish but they look great on top of the gumbo.

INGREDIENT TIP: Make this dish even heartier by adding ¼ pound of chopped bacon or sliced smoked andouille sausage. Sauté the bacon or sausage with the holy trinity.

SERVING TIP: Serve over cooked rice for a classic comfort food dinner.

PER SERVING: Calories: 174; Total fat: 8g; Protein: 17g; Carbohydrates: 10g; Fiber: 2g; Sugar: 2g; Sodium: 221mg

OPEN-FACED TUNA MELTS

NUT-FREE / 30 MINUTES / ONE POT
SERVES 2 / PREP TIME: 10 MINUTES / COOK TIME: 10 MINUTES

In 1965, the tuna melt became popular in the United States when it was "accidentally" served at a Woolworth's lunch counter to a customer who ordered a grilled cheese sandwich. Some are made as closed sandwiches, but I prefer this open-faced version. Reserve a pinch of the parsley for garnish.

2 tablespoons unsalted butter, at room temperature

2 slices sourdough bread

1 can oil-packed tuna, drained and oil reserved

½ small shallot, finely minced

1 stalk celery, finely minced

½ cup quartered grape tomatoes

1 tablespoon coarsely chopped flat leaf parsley, plus additional for garnish

Pinch kosher salt

Pinch freshly ground black pepper

3 tablespoons mayonnaise

1 teaspoon Dijon mustard

2 slices Monterey Jack or Provolone cheese

1. Turn on the broiler.

2. Heat a nonstick skillet over medium heat. Spread the butter on one side of the sliced bread and when the pan is hot, place the slices in the pan butter side down. When the underside takes on a crispy, golden color, transfer to a baking sheet lined with foil, placing the toasts crispy side down.

3. In a medium bowl, mix together the tuna, shallot, celery, tomatoes, parsley, salt, pepper, mayonnaise, and mustard.

4. To assemble the melts, drizzle 1 or 2 teaspoons of the reserved tuna oil over the toasts, then divide the tuna mixture between them. Spread the mixture evenly across the toasts right to the edges. Place a slice of cheese on top of each.

5. Slide the tray under the broiler for 1 minute, or until the cheese begins to melt and browns slightly.

6. Remove from the broiler and garnish with a pinch of parsley. Transfer the melts to plates and serve.

INGREDIENT TIP: Substitute canned salmon, roughly chopped cooked shrimp, or crabmeat for the tuna; or make it extra indulgent with chopped lobster meat and Gruyère cheese.

PER SERVING: Calories: 525; Total fat: 38g; Protein: 17g; Carbohydrates: 25g; Fiber: 2g; Sugar: 6g; Sodium: 753mg

SMOKED OYSTER SOUP

GLUTEN-FREE / NUT-FREE / ONE POT
SERVES 6 TO 8 / PREP TIME: 15 MINUTES / COOK TIME: 25 MINUTES

This soup reminds me of an oyster soup served for a New Year's celebration in one of the *Little House on the Prairie* books written by Laura Ingalls Wilder. She talks about the creamy-salty combination of the soup and how she ate every last drop from her bowl and was disappointed when it was all gone. I'm disappointed when this soup is gone, too.

6 slices Applewood smoked bacon, cut into ¼-inch strips

1 medium yellow onion, cut into ¼-inch cubes

1 leek, white part only, rinsed thoroughly and sliced thin

Kosher salt

1 tablespoon Old Bay seasoning

1 large russet potato, peeled and cut into ½-inch cubes

½ cup half and half

1 quart whole milk

1 (4-ounce) bottle clam juice

1 pint fresh shucked oysters

1 can smoked oysters

Crackers or croutons, for serving

1. In a Dutch oven over medium heat, cook the bacon until lightly brown, about 4 to 6 minutes.

2. Add the onion and leek, and sauté until softened, another 4 to 6 minutes, stirring often. Season the vegetables with a pinch of salt and add the Old Bay seasoning.

3. Add the potato, half and half, milk, and clam juice, and bring to a boil. Lower the heat to medium and simmer uncovered until the potato is tender, 8 to 10 minutes.

4. Add both types of oysters and gently simmer until the fresh oysters are just cooked, about 2 minutes. Taste, and season with salt as needed.

5. Serve the soup hot in warmed soup bowls with crackers or croutons.

PREPARATION TIP: Cook the soup base (steps 1 through 3) a few days ahead of time and reheat it just to a simmer before adding the oysters. Letting the soup sit in the refrigerator allows it to develop a deeper flavor.

PER SERVING: Calories: 284; Total fat: 13g; Protein: 11g; Carbohydrates: 27g; Fiber: 2g; Sugar: 11g; Sodium: 727mg

SPICY THAI COCONUT SHRIMP SOUP

GLUTEN-FREE / DAIRY-FREE / NUT-FREE / ONE POT
SERVES 4 / PREP TIME: 15 MINUTES / COOK TIME: 25 MINUTES

The key in this recipe is to be mindful of how much red curry paste you use. It's a very spicy base in Thai cooking, and a little can go a long way. If you find it too hot, balance it out with more sugar and lime juice.

2 tablespoons coconut oil

2 stalks lemongrass, peeled down to the core, smashed flat, and finely minced

3 garlic cloves, finely minced

1-inch piece fresh ginger, finely minced

1 large red bell pepper, cut into ½-inch cubes

Pinch kosher salt

2 tablespoons red curry paste

1 (13½-ounce) can coconut milk

Zest of 1 lime

Juice of 1 lime

1 tablespoon brown sugar

1 cup water

1 pound medium shrimp (41–50 shrimp per pound), peeled and deveined

1 tablespoon fish sauce (optional)

1 lime cut into 4 wedges, for serving

2 tablespoons roughly chopped cilantro, divided

2 cups cooked white rice

Sliced scallions, for garnish

1. In a medium saucepan or Dutch oven, melt the coconut oil over medium-high heat. Sauté the lemongrass, garlic, and ginger until fragrant, 2 to 3 minutes.

2. Add the bell pepper and cook for 3 minutes more, or until soft. Add the salt. You may need to turn the heat down to keep the aromatics from burning. Add the curry paste and stir quickly to sauté and combine with the vegetables, about 1 minute.

3. Add the coconut milk, lime zest, lime juice, and brown sugar, and stir 1 cup of water into the pot. Reduce the heat to medium-low and simmer, stirring occasionally, for about 5 minutes.

4. Season the shrimp with the fish sauce (if using, or use a pinch of salt) and add to the soup. Simmer for 10 to 12 minutes, or until the shrimp are pink and opaque. Turn off the heat and stir in 1 tablespoon of cilantro.

5. To serve, evenly divide the cooked rice among 4 warmed soup bowls. Divide the soup and shrimp among the bowls and top with remaining 1 tablespoon of cilantro. Serve with the lime wedges, and for an extra pop of color, garnish with sliced scallions.

SUBSTITUTION TIP: Crabmeat makes an excellent substitution here; and you can also switch the red curry paste for a milder, sweeter yellow curry paste.

PER SERVING: Calories: 524; Total fat: 28g; Protein: 25g; Carbohydrates: 40g; Fiber: 1g; Sugar: 5g; Sodium: 658mg

LOBSTER ROLL

NUT-FREE
SERVES 4 / PREP TIME: 45 MINUTES / COOK TIME: 10 MINUTES

I worked at a cooking school that was located above an upscale gourmet grocery store. For my colleague's birthday, every year I would make her whatever she wanted for lunch. One year, she chose a lobster roll. She's told me a few times over the years that it was the best lobster roll she'd ever had. And now, it can be your best one, too!

4 (1-pound) live lobsters, or 2 pounds cooked lobster meat

¼ cup kosher salt, plus a pinch

⅓ cup mayonnaise

1 teaspoon Old Bay seasoning

Pinch freshly ground pepper

Zest of 1 lemon

Juice of 1 lemon

2 or 3 tender celery stalks (the inner stalks toward the center), cut into ¼-inch cubes

4 top-split hot dog buns or sandwich rolls

2 tablespoons unsalted butter, melted

4 leaves Bibb lettuce, shredded

1. Cook the lobsters by first dispatching them. Use the tip of a very sharp and heavy chef knife and drive the tip straight into the crack on the head, behind the eyes. Set up an ice water bath in a large bowl and set aside. Bring a large stock pot of water to a rolling boil and add ¼ cup of salt. Cook the lobsters until they turn bright red, about 5 minutes. Using tongs, lift the lobsters from the water and immediately plunge them into the ice water bath. Chill them for about 5 minutes, then drain the water.

2. When the lobsters are cold, remove the tails and claws and discard the bodies (or use for another recipe). Crack the shells using seafood crackers or sharp shears and remove the meat. Trim out the vein that runs down the tail and cut the meat into ½-inch chunks. Place the meat on top of a strainer set over a bowl to catch the excess liquid, and chill in the refrigerator for at least 30 minutes.

3. In a large mixing bowl, combine the lobster meat with the mayonnaise, Old Bay seasoning, salt, pepper, lemon zest, lemon juice (reserving 1 or 2 teaspoons for drizzling over the rolls), and celery. Taste, and adjust the seasoning. Cover and refrigerate until ready to assemble.

CONTINUED ▸

4. Heat a large nonstick skillet over medium heat. Brush the hot dog buns with melted butter and lay them flat in the skillet, toasting until golden brown. Place each bun on a warmed plate and line with the Bibb lettuce, then spoon in the lobster salad. Drizzle with the reserved lemon juice and serve.

PREPARATION TIP: In order to get the most delicious and fresh lobster meat possible, you must start with a live lobster. If you'd rather skip this step, simply use 2 pounds of cooked lobster meat instead.

SUBSTITUTION TIP: As if lobster in a sandwich weren't already indulgent enough, swap it for some succulent prawns or scallops. Sauté or broil the prawns or sear the scallops before folding them into the salad.

PER SERVING: Calories: 587; Total fat: 24g; Protein: 59g; Carbohydrates: 31g; Fiber: 1g; Sugar: 7g; Sodium: 1,348mg

SALMON BURGERS

NUT-FREE / ONE POT
SERVES 4 / PREP TIME: 40 MINUTES / COOK TIME: 10 MINUTES

If you want to give up red meat for a while—which wouldn't be a bad idea in the spirit of practicing sustainability—you can still have a decadent, juicy burger using salmon! Salmon's naturally oily mouthfeel can satisfy a burger craving while at the same time helping to cut down on saturated fats and increase your omega-3 intake.

FOR THE BURGERS

- 1½ pounds salmon fillet, skin removed and roughly chopped into ¼-inch pieces
- 1 small shallot, grated
- 2 teaspoons capers, rinsed and finely chopped
- 1 tablespoon minced flat leaf parsley
- Zest of 1 lemon
- 2 teaspoons freshly squeezed lemon juice
- 1 teaspoon Dijon mustard
- ½ cup mayonnaise
- Pinch kosher salt
- Pinch freshly ground black pepper
- ¾ cup panko bread crumbs, divided
- 2 tablespoons unsalted butter
- 4 brioche hamburger buns, toasted
- 1 cup arugula leaves
- 4 tomato slices

TO MAKE THE BURGERS

1. In a mixing bowl, combine the salmon, shallot, capers, parsley, lemon zest, lemon juice, Dijon mustard, mayonnaise, and salt and pepper. Mix well, then cover with plastic wrap and refrigerate for 30 minutes (or overnight).

2. Mix in ½ cup of bread crumbs and form 4 equal-size patties, about 1 inch thick. Press the remaining ¼ cup bread crumbs into the patties on each side.

3. In a large nonstick skillet over medium-high heat, melt the butter. Cook the salmon patties for about 4 minutes per side, just until the patties become golden brown. Transfer the patties to a warmed plate and tent with foil. Rest them for about 5 minutes while you prepare the sauce.

TO MAKE THE SAUCE

4. Stir together the mayonnaise, Dijon mustard, lemon juice to taste, dill, and a pinch each of salt and pepper. Spread the sauce on the bottom pieces of the brioche buns and divide the arugula equally among each. Top with a sliced tomato, then a salmon patty. Spread more sauce on the top bun and place the bun on the patty. Serve immediately.

CONTINUED ▸

FOR THE SAUCE

¼ cup mayonnaise

1 teaspoon Dijon mustard

4 to 6 teaspoons freshly
squeezed lemon juice

2 teaspoons finely minced
fresh dill

Pinch kosher salt

Pinch freshly ground
black pepper

SERVING TIP: Make it a "California style" burger and add sliced avocado to each sandwich.

SUBSTITUTION TIP: Any fish fillet can make an outstanding burger patty. I like to chop up leftover raw tuna fillet for burgers if I don't have salmon on hand.

PER SERVING: Calories: 729; Total fat: 41g; Protein: 42g; Carbohydrates: 47g; Fiber: 2g; Sugar: 11g; Sodium: 810mg

CIOPPINO

GLUTEN-FREE / DAIRY-FREE / NUT-FREE / ONE POT
SERVES 4 / PREP TIME: 15 MINUTES / COOK TIME: 40 MINUTES

What started as a humble tomato-based stew for fishermen using scraps of fish turned into a recipe that is quintessentially San Francisco. The crab used in cioppino is typically Dungeness, but any type of crab that is available will work perfectly. Accordingly, any combination of finfish and shellfish works beautifully in this stew. Serve with garlic bread for a delectable, hearty meal.

2 tablespoons extra-virgin olive oil

Pinch red pepper flakes

1 small yellow onion, cut into ¼-inch cubes

1 small fennel bulb, trimmed and cut into ¼-inch cubes, feathery fronds reserved for garnish

2 garlic cloves, thinly sliced

Kosher salt

Freshly ground black pepper

2 tablespoons tomato paste

¼ cup dry white wine

1 (14-ounce) can diced tomatoes

2 cups fish or shellfish broth

¼ pound salmon fillet, cut into 2-inch pieces

¼ pound bay scallops

12 large shrimp (31–35 shrimp per pound), peeled and deveined

16 clams, cleaned

16 mussels, cleaned

1 (2-pound) scrubbed Dungeness crab, top shell removed and body cut into quarters

1. In a Dutch oven over medium heat, add the olive oil and red pepper flakes. Sweat the onion, fennel, and garlic in the oil by placing a lid on the pot while it heats up, 4 to 6 minutes, stirring occasionally.

2. Remove the lid and add a pinch each of salt and pepper. Continue to cook uncovered until the liquid has evaporated, about another 2 minutes.

3. Add the tomato paste and sauté for 3 minutes. Add the wine and cook for another 5 minutes, or until the wine has almost evaporated. Add the diced tomatoes and fish broth, and increase the heat to medium-high, bringing to a boil. Reduce the heat to medium-low. Simmer for 10 minutes to reduce the liquid slightly and concentrate the flavors.

4. Add the salmon, scallops, shrimp, clams, mussels, and crab to the pot. Season with salt and pepper, and gently fold the seafood in to combine with the tomato stew. Cover and cook for 8 to 10 minutes on medium-low heat, or until all the seafood is cooked.

5. To serve, divide the cioppino among 4 warmed soup bowls and garnish with the reserved fennel fronds. Serve hot.

CONTINUED ▶

PREPARATION TIP: The tomato stew base can be made ahead of time, cooled, and kept in the refrigerator for up to 4 days. In fact, the flavor develops beautifully if you make the stew even one day ahead. Bring the stew to a boil, then reduce the heat to a simmer and cook the seafood.

SERVING TIP: Make a heartier stew by adding some diced potatoes, or spoon the stew over cooked pasta shells.

PER SERVING: Calories: 322; Total fat: 10g; Protein: 38g; Carbohydrates: 17g; Fiber: 4g; Sugar: 5g; Sodium: 1,062mg

BOUILLABAISSE

NUT-FREE / ONE POT
SERVES 4 / PREP TIME: 20 MINUTES / COOK TIME: 35 MINUTES

This hearty and aromatic seafood stew originated in the Provence region of France, specifically in the port city of Marseille. The aromatics used in this recipe represent influences from all parts of the Mediterranean, including North Africa, Spain, and Greece. Pernod is an anise-flavored liqueur from the south of France that adds a wonderful aroma to the dish, but it's optional to include.

FOR THE BOUILLABAISSE

2 tablespoons unsalted butter

**2 large shallots,
   coarsely chopped**

**2 garlic cloves,
   coarsely chopped**

Zest of 1 orange

**1 teaspoon fennel
   seeds, toasted**

1 bay leaf

**Generous pinch saffron
   threads, crushed**

**2 tablespoons Pernod
   (optional)**

**1 (14-ounce) can diced
   tomatoes**

4 cups seafood broth

**1 large Yukon Gold potato,
   cut into ½-inch cubes**

**1½ pounds whitefish (like red
   snapper or cod), skinned,
   deboned, and cut into
   1½-inch pieces**

TO MAKE THE BOUILLABAISSE

1. Melt the butter in a large Dutch oven over medium heat. Add the shallots and sauté, stirring occasionally until translucent, about 6 minutes. Add the garlic and continue to sauté until the garlic is soft, another 2 minutes. Add the orange zest, fennel seeds, bay leaf, and saffron threads, and cook until fragrant, about 1 minute.

2. Add the Pernod (if using) and cook until it reduces by half, about 3 minutes, stirring occasionally. Add the tomatoes, seafood broth, and potato. Bring the mixture to a simmer and cook on medium heat for about 10 minutes, or until the stew begins to thicken.

3. Add the whitefish and gently stir, cooking for 5 to 6 minutes. Add the shrimp and gently stir, cooking for 2 minutes. Add the mussels and gently stir, then cover and cook for another 3 to 4 minutes.

4. Uncover the pot and discard any unopened mussels (if they don't open, it means they were dead before cooking and are bad). Taste and adjust the seasoning with salt and pepper. Reduce the heat to low and continue to simmer gently while you make the rouille.

CONTINUED ▶

¼ pound medium shrimp
   (41–50 shrimp per pound),
   peeled and deveined

¼ pound mussels, scrubbed
   and debearded

Kosher salt

Freshly ground black pepper

FOR THE ROUILLE

1 (4-ounce) jar diced pimentos, drained

1 garlic clove, chopped

½ teaspoon kosher salt

Zest of 1 lemon

Juice of 1 lemon

2 (¼-inch-thick) slices French
   baguette

¼ cup extra-virgin olive oil

FOR SERVING

1 French baguette, sliced into
   ¼-inch-thick rounds, toasted

TO MAKE THE ROUILLE

5. Add the pimentos, garlic, salt, lemon zest, and lemon juice
   to a blender and process until smooth. Dip the bread slices
   into the stew briefly to absorb some of the stew and add to
   the blender. With the motor running, drizzle in the olive oil
   until the rouille is smooth and looks thick, like mayonnaise.

TO SERVE

6. Remove the bay leaf. Divide the seafood and tomato broth
   among 4 warmed soup bowls. Top with a toasted baguette
   slice and a dollop of rouille. Serve hot.

PREPARATION TIP: The richer and more flavorful the broth,
the better the stew! Save up on shells from your crab, lobster, and
shrimp dishes and keep them in a container in your freezer. Roast
your saved shells, then simmer them for 20 to 30 minutes in fish
or seafood broth for even more flavor.

PER SERVING: Calories: 789; Total fat: 24g; Protein: 66g; Carbohydrates:
74g; Fiber: 4g; Sugar: 4g; Sodium: 1,974mg

SHRIMP BANH MI SANDWICHES

NUT-FREE / ONE POT
SERVES 4 / PREP TIME: 15 MINUTES, PLUS 10 MINUTES TO MARINATE /
COOK TIME: 10 MINUTES

Think of these as po' boy sandwiches with a Vietnamese twist. The French baguette was introduced to Vietnamese cuisine in the mid-nineteenth century, and by the 1950s, these sandwiches had become a common Vietnamese street food. A fusion of Vietnamese and French cuisine, *banh mi* technically means "bread" in Vietnamese, but if you order a banh mi they'll understand you mean the entire sandwich.

½ **small shallot, finely minced**

1 **small stalk lemongrass, peeled down to its core, smashed, and finely minced**

1 **teaspoon brown sugar**

Zest of 1 lime

Juice of 1 lime

2 **tablespoons fish sauce**

Small pinch red pepper flakes

12 **jumbo raw shrimp (21–25), peeled and deveined**

3 **tablespoons mayonnaise**

2 **tablespoons vegetable oil**

4 **French sandwich rolls, toasted**

2 **medium carrots, peeled and sliced, or grated into thin matchsticks**

½ **English cucumber, thinly sliced diagonally**

1 **or 2 small jalapeños, thinly sliced**

½ **bunch cilantro, stems trimmed**

1. In a small bowl, stir together the shallot, lemongrass, brown sugar, lime zest, lime juice, fish sauce, and red pepper flakes. Put the shrimp in a medium bowl, pour half the mixture over the shrimp, and toss. Marinate for about 10 minutes, but no more than 30 minutes, as shrimp marinate quickly and can get salty and tough if marinated too long. Add the mayonnaise to the remaining mixture not used to marinate the shrimp, and stir to combine.

2. Heat a nonstick skillet over medium-high heat and add the oil. When the oil is just starting to smoke, add the shrimp, shaking off as much of the marinade as possible before placing the shrimp in the pan. Cook the shrimp for 3 to 4 minutes, flipping halfway through, or until they turn opaque and firm (but not rubbery). Transfer the shrimp to a plate and tent with foil.

3. Spread the seasoned mayonnaise on both sides of each French roll. Divide the carrots and cucumber between the rolls, then place 3 shrimp on the rolls per sandwich. Top each sandwich with the jalapeño slices and cilantro. Place each sandwich on a warmed plate and serve hot.

CONTINUED ▸

INGREDIENT TIP: Lemongrass is an aromatic herb widely used in Southeast Asian cuisines. The center core is the only part to be used in cooking, though the outer peelings can be used to infuse teas, soups, or even added to the pot when steaming rice. Peel the layers away until you reach the smooth center core. Lay the core on a cutting board and with the flat part of the knife blade, smash the core flat, then proceed with mincing.

PER SERVING: Calories: 433; Total fat: 18g; Protein: 19g; Carbohydrates: 49g; Fiber: 3g; Sugar: 9g; Sodium: 1,308mg

SARDINE AND PIMENTO BOCADILLOS

DAIRY-FREE / NUT-FREE / 30 MINUTE
SERVES 4 / PREP TIME: 10 MINUTES / COOK TIME: 5 MINUTES

The *bocadillo* is an iconic Spanish street food sandwich typically made by layering thin slices of ham and cheese in a split baguette. You can walk down any street in Spain and find a cafe selling bocadillos along with wine and coffee. I couldn't resist turning this recipe into a version of my favorite Spanish tapa: *pan con tomate*—toasted baguette rubbed with garlic and tomato.

1 soft French baguette, split in half lengthwise

1 large garlic clove, peeled

1 small Roma tomato, cut in half

3 tablespoons extra-virgin olive oil

Kosher salt

Freshly ground black pepper

1 (4-ounce) can oil-packed sardines, oil reserved

1 (4-ounce) jar sliced pimentos, drained

1. Set your oven broiler to high. Line a baking sheet with foil.

2. Place the baguette cut side up on the prepared baking sheet. Toast the bread under the broiler for 2 minutes, or until the surface becomes golden. Leave the broiler on.

3. Lightly rub the garlic over the toasted surface and then follow with the tomato, pressing lightly to smear some of the tomato juices and pulp onto the bread. Save the garlic and tomato to use for another recipe or chop them up and eat them on toast with a little olive oil.

4. Drizzle the olive oil over the bread and season lightly with the salt and pepper. Place the sardines on top of one side of the baguette, then top with the pimentos. Drizzle 1 or 2 teaspoons of the reserved sardine oil over the pimentos.

5. Broil the sandwich for another 2 to 3 minutes to heat the sardines and pimentos. Remove from the broiler and close up the sandwich. Cut the sandwich into 4 equal pieces and serve.

SUBSTITUTION TIP: You can use oil-packed canned tuna or smoked mackerel instead of sardines.

PER SERVING: Calories: 411; Total fat: 14g; Protein: 17g; Carbohydrates: 55g; Fiber: 3g; Sugar: 3g; Sodium: 663mg

PAN BAGNAT (PROVENÇAL TUNA SANDWICHES)

NUT-FREE / NO COOK

SERVES 4 / PREP TIME: 20 MINUTES, PLUS 15 MINUTES TO CHILL

Part tuna sandwich, part tuna niçoise salad, *pan bagnat* (pan ban-yah) is cousin to the Italian *muffuletta* sandwich that hails from New Orleans. Indeed, the south of France is a world away from Louisiana, but the Italian immigrants who settled in New Orleans probably had Mediterranean roots, just like this Provençal sandwich.

¼ cup olive tapenade spread

1 small garlic clove,
    finely minced

1 small shallot, finely minced

2 oil-packed anchovy fillets,
    finely chopped

1 cup parsley leaves with
    tender stems,
    coarsely chopped

1 tablespoon red wine vinegar

1 tablespoon Dijon mustard

3 tablespoons extra-virgin
    olive oil, divided

1 (5-ounce) can oil-packed
    tuna, drained and oil
    reserved

1 French baguette, split
    lengthwise and
    lightly toasted

2 large hardboiled eggs, peeled
    and thinly sliced

1 large Roma tomato, sliced
    into ¼-inch thick rounds

2 roasted red peppers from a
    jar, sliced into thin strips

Freshly ground black pepper

1. In a small bowl, mix together the tapenade, garlic, shallot, anchovies, and parsley. Stir in the red wine vinegar and Dijon mustard. Drizzle in 1 tablespoon of olive oil and stir to combine.

2. Drizzle 2 teaspoons of the reserved tuna oil over each cut side of the baguette. Spread the tapenade mixture on both sides of the bread. Then top with the tuna. Top the tuna with alternating slices of the egg and tomato, then top with the red peppers. Drizzle the remaining 2 tablespoons of olive oil over the top and season with pepper.

3. Wrap the sandwich tightly in foil and cut in half. Wrap again in another piece of foil or plastic wrap and place the halves side by side. Weigh the sandwiches down with something heavy, like a cast iron skillet or Dutch oven. Refrigerate for 10 to 15 minutes.

4. Unwrap the sandwiches and cut in half again to serve.

PREPARATION TIP: You can leave the sandwich in the refrigerator overnight to press and marinate, but let it come to room temperature before serving so the flavors really shine.

INGREDIENT TIP: Any leftover finfish you have from another recipe will work beautifully in this sandwich.

PER SERVING: Calories: 645; Total fat: 22g; Protein: 29g; Carbohydrates: 83g; Fiber: 6g; Sugar: 3g; Sodium: 3,049mg

TROUT HAND PIES

NUT-FREE
SERVES 4 / PREP TIME: 1 HOUR / COOK TIME: 50 MINUTES

Similar to empanadas, these savory pies are extra tasty and make a great lunch paired with a salad. They would also be great to tuck into a picnic basket. The recipe is a little time consuming, but have faith: The frozen puff pastry is there to save you time.

FOR THE FILLING

6 tablespoons (¾ stick) unsalted butter, at room temperature

1 small shallot, finely minced

1 pound trout fillets, deboned, skinned, and cut into 2-inch chunks (trout is typically deboned when you buy it, and skinning the fillets is quick work)

Kosher salt

Freshly ground black pepper

1 small russet potato, cooked and cut into ¼-inch cubes

2 tablespoons sour cream

1 tablespoon finely chopped flat leaf parsley

1 tablespoon finely chopped dill

Zest of 1 lemon

Juice of 1 lemon

1 large egg white

TO MAKE THE FILLING

1. In a large nonstick skillet over medium heat, melt the butter and sauté the shallot until translucent, about 4 minutes. While the shallot is cooking, lightly season the trout with a pinch each of salt and pepper. Cook half the trout pieces, about 6 minutes, flipping halfway through. Transfer the cooked fish to a mixing bowl and repeat with the remaining fish. Transfer all the butter, shallots, and fish to the bowl and cool the fish to room temperature.

2. When the fish is cool, flake with a fork until you have random-size chunks and flakes. Stir in the potato, sour cream, parsley, dill, lemon zest, and lemon juice. Season with salt and pepper, and stir to combine; the mixture should be thick and paste-like.

3. In a small bowl, whisk the egg white until foamy and fold it into the mixture. Cover and refrigerate for about 30 minutes.

TO MAKE THE PUFF PASTRY

4. Preheat the oven to 400°F and line a baking sheet with parchment paper.

FOR THE PUFF PASTRY

One package frozen puff pastry (2 sheets per package), thawed in the refrigerator

¼ cup all-purpose flour, for dusting

1 large egg, beaten with 1 teaspoon water

½ tablespoon flaky sea salt

5. Remove the puff pastry from the refrigerator. Dust your work surface and rolling pin with a bit of flour and roll one sheet of puff pastry out to a roughly 12-by-16-inch rectangle. Cut the pastry in half to create two pieces that are each about 8-by-12 inches. Repeat this process with the second pastry. Fold each piece in half like a book to make a crease, then unfold.

6. Divide the filling into fourths and place each portion in the center of the right side of each pastry, spreading it slightly but leaving a half-inch edge around the perimeter. Fold the left side of the pastry over and line up the edges. Use a fork to crimp the edges all around the pastry and place the pies on the prepared sheet pan.

7. Brush the tops of the pies with the beaten egg and sprinkle the tops with a small pinch of salt. Cut two 1-inch-long slits on the top of each pie. Wrap the pies in plastic wrap and chill in the freezer for 20 minutes, or until the pastry feels firm.

8. Remove from the freezer and discard the plastic wrap. Bake until golden brown, about 35 to 40 minutes. Transfer the pies to a wire cooling rack and cool for at least 20 minutes. Serve warm.

PREPARATION TIP: For the flakiest crust, refrigerate the assembled pies overnight before baking them. By keeping the pastry as cold as possible before baking, the fats in the pastry take longer to melt, which gives you a flakier pastry.

INGREDIENT TIP: You can use cooked salmon, tuna, or catfish in place of the trout for these pies. Canned, fresh, or even leftover fish from last night's dinner works great for the filling!

PER SERVING: Calories: 888; Total fat: 59g; Protein: 37g; Carbohydrates: 53g; Fiber: 3g; Sugar: 2g; Sodium: 1,192mg

Grilled Shrimp Kabobs
with Pesto Sauce, page 130

CHAPTER 5

ENTRÉES

I LOVE THIS collection of entrée recipes—there's something for every palate, and I've included many classics as well as some original dishes of my own. We all get busy during the week, but there isn't anything nicer you can do for yourself than to make a home-cooked meal. Save yourself some time and buy precut vegetables to store in the refrigerator for when you need them; that makes for easy dinner prep!

CLASSIC BRITISH FISH AND CHIPS

DAIRY-FREE / NUT-FREE / ONE POT
SERVES 2 / PREP TIME: 20 MINUTES, PLUS 30 MINUTES TO LET SOAK / COOK TIME: 30 MINUTES

There are two secrets for the best fish and chips: (1) Maintain the oil temperature between 365°F and 375°F for a perfect light and crispy texture; and (2) fry the chips twice—once to cook, and the second time for texture and color.

FOR THE CHIPS

2 large russet potatoes, peeled and cut into strips about 1 inch thick by 1½ inches wide

1½ quarts vegetable oil, for frying

Kosher salt

FOR THE FISH

¾ cup all-purpose flour, divided

¼ cup rice flour

¼ cup cornstarch

1 teaspoon baking powder

½ teaspoon cayenne pepper

Pinch kosher salt

⅓ cup beer (such as Newcastle Brown Ale)

⅓ cup sparkling water

2 (6-ounce) haddock or cod fillets, each cut into 3 equal pieces

Malt vinegar, for serving

Lemon wedges, for serving

TO MAKE THE CHIPS

1. Soak the potatoes in a bowl of cold water for up to 30 minutes.

2. Heat the oil in a large Dutch oven over medium-high heat to 365°F. If you don't have an instant-read thermometer, dip a wooden spoon handle or chopstick into the oil—the oil is ready when it bubbles and sizzles around the wood.

3. Drain the water from the potatoes and blot them dry with paper towels.

4. Using a wire skimmer, gently lower the potatoes into the oil. Fry for 7 to 8 minutes, or until translucent and soft. Test a potato strip by piercing it with a fork—it should easily puncture the potato. Using the skimmer, transfer the potatoes to a wire rack set over a sheet pan.

5. Bring the oil back to 365°F and test the temperature using a thermometer or the wooden spoon trick. Fry the chips a second time for 3 to 5 minutes. When they're golden brown and crispy, transfer them to a wire cooling rack and turn off the heat. Season the chips lightly with salt.

TO MAKE THE FISH

6. In a medium mixing bowl, prepare the batter by combining ¼ cup of flour, the rice flour, the cornstarch, the baking powder, the cayenne, and the salt. Whisk in the beer and sparkling water until a light, foamy batter develops and the mixture is smooth.

7. Reheat the oil in the Dutch oven to 375°F. Blot the fish dry with paper towels and lightly season both sides with salt. Place the remaining flour on a wide plate and dredge the fish to coat evenly. Shake off the excess and dip it into the batter, coating the fish evenly.

8. Test the oil by adding a drop of batter. If it sizzles and immediately floats to the surface, the oil is ready. Use tongs to gently lower the fish into the oil. Cook in batches, up to 3 pieces at a time. Fry for 6 to 8 minutes, flipping halfway through, or until golden brown and crispy. Keep an eye on the oil and adjust the heat if needed to maintain consistent temperature. Use a wire skimmer to transfer the fish to a paper towel–lined plate.

9. Serve the fish and chips on a warm platter and drizzle some malt vinegar over with a squeeze of lemon juice. Serve hot.

COOKING TIP: Overcrowding can cool the oil, making the food dense and soggy. Fry in smaller batches for perfect golden crispiness.

PRO TIP: Save and reuse the oil. Cool to room temperature, strain, store in a sealable container, and label "fish-frying oil." Reuse to make fish and chips again, or for pan frying or searing fish and seafood.

PER SERVING: Calories: 1,744; Total fat: 110g; Protein: 52g; Carbohydrates: 135g; Fiber: 7g; Sugar: 2g; Sodium: 396mg

SPICY FIDEOS WITH MUSSELS

DAIRY-FREE / NUT-FREE / ONE POT
SERVES 4 / PREP TIME: 15 MINUTES / COOK TIME: 25 MINUTES

Originating in Catalonia, fideos are thin, short pasta noodles used in this dish, which is similar to paella but cooks in less time and is a bit lighter. The key to the fideos' texture is to fry them lightly before adding the stock. This is a great party dish, so invite friends over and open the wine!

4 tablespoons extra-virgin olive oil, divided

1 shallot, finely minced

4 garlic cloves, finely minced

Generous pinch red pepper flakes

½ pound dried fideo noodles

Kosher salt

Freshly ground pepper

1 Roma tomato, diced

1 tablespoon tomato paste

Generous pinch saffron threads

2 teaspoons smoked paprika

1½ cups fish or shrimp broth

1½ pounds mussels, scrubbed

Juice of 1 lemon

Chopped parsley, for garnish (optional)

1. In a large enameled cast iron skillet or paella pan, heat the oil over medium heat until shimmering. Add the shallot, garlic, red pepper flakes, and fideos. Season with salt and pepper, and cook, stirring occasionally, until the fideos are lightly toasted, about 5 minutes.

2. Add the diced tomato, tomato paste, saffron, and paprika. Sauté until lightly caramelized, about 3 minutes. Stir in the fish broth and bring to a simmer. Continue to simmer, stirring often, over medium-low heat until the pasta is al dente, about 5 to 6 minutes.

3. Debeard the mussels by pulling off any fibrous clumps hanging from the shells, using your fingers or a pair of tweezers. Pick through the mussels, tapping any open shells lightly against the counter. If the shells do not close up in response, they are not fresh and should be discarded. Stir in the mussels, cover, and cook over low heat until they open, 8 to 10 minutes.

4. Remove from the heat and discard any mussels that have not opened (this means they were dead before cooking and should not be eaten). Drizzle with lemon juice and serve hot. Garnish with a little chopped parsley (if using).

PREPARATION TIP: This dish tastes better the next day when the flavors have had time to develop. Double the recipe so you have leftovers!

INGREDIENT TIP: If fideos are not available, substitute thin angel hair pasta and break into 2- to 3-inch pieces.

PER SERVING: Calories: 584; Total fat: 21g; Protein: 37g; Carbohydrates: 63g; Fiber: 3g; Sugar: 5g; Sodium: 711mg

BANG BANG SHRIMP IN LETTUCE CUPS

GLUTEN-FREE / NUT-FREE / 30 MINUTE / ONE POT
SERVES 2 TO 4 / PREP TIME: 15 MINUTES, PLUS 10 MINUTES TO MARINATE / COOK TIME: 10 MINUTES

Bang bang shrimp is a very popular dish in many restaurants across the country. I like to serve the shrimp in lettuce cups with a simple slaw for a light supper.

FOR THE SAUCE

¼ cup Sriracha sauce

¼ cup plain Greek yogurt

¼ cup mayonnaise

2 tablespoons Thai sweet chili sauce

FOR THE SLAW

½ cup shredded red cabbage

¼ cup shredded carrot

2 scallions, white and green parts thinly sliced

¼ bunch cilantro, roughly chopped

Juice of 1 lime

Pinch kosher salt

FOR THE SHRIMP

1 pound large shrimp (31–35 shrimp per pound), peeled and deveined

½ cup buttermilk

1 teaspoon Sriracha

1½ cups vegetable oil

½ cup cornstarch

Kosher salt

8 Bibb lettuce leaves, trimmed into cups

Chopped cilantro, for garnish (optional)

TO MAKE THE SAUCE

1. In a small bowl, stir together the Sriracha, Greek yogurt, mayonnaise, and Thai chili sauce. Set aside.

TO MAKE THE SLAW

2. Toss together the cabbage, carrot, scallions, and cilantro with the lime juice. Season with the salt and set aside.

TO MAKE THE SHRIMP

3. In a medium bowl, toss the shrimp in the buttermilk with the Sriracha. Marinate for 10 minutes.

4. While the shrimp are marinating, heat the oil in a cast iron skillet over medium-high heat. Remove the shrimp from the buttermilk, shake off the excess, and coat with the cornstarch.

5. When the oil reaches 365°F, fry the shrimp for 2 to 3 minutes per side until golden brown. Transfer to a paper towel–lined plate and season lightly with salt.

6. Toss the shrimp in the sauce and divide among the lettuce cups. Top with the slaw. Garnish with cilantro (if using) to brighten the flavors. Serve immediately.

VARIATION TIP: I chose to lighten the sauce by using half yogurt, half mayo, but you can certainly go for all mayo if you want to.

PER SERVING: Calories: 1,161; Total fat: 79g; Protein: 53g; Carbohydrates: 55g; Fiber: 2g; Sugar: 22g; Sodium: 1,421mg

BROILED SHRIMP SCAMPI WITH CRUMBLED BACON

NUT-FREE / 30 MINUTE / ONE POT
SERVES 4 / PREP TIME: 15 MINUTES / COOK TIME: 10 MINUTES

Butterflying the shrimp isn't necessary, but it does flatten them so they cook faster, look bigger, and carry more of the butter and bacon. It takes just a few extra moments, and it's totally worth it. See the Preparation tip for how to butterfly the shrimp.

1 tablespoon extra-virgin olive oil

4 tablespoons unsalted butter, at room temperature

5 garlic cloves, finely minced

Pinch of crushed red pepper flakes

Zest of 1 lemon

⅓ cup chopped parsley, divided

Kosher salt

Freshly ground black pepper

1½ pounds colossal shrimp (under 15 shrimp per pound), shelled, deveined, and butterflied

½ pound bacon, finely chopped and cooked to crispy brown bits

Juice of 1 lemon

Crusty bread, for serving

1. Set the broiler to high. Line a baking sheet with foil and grease the foil with the olive oil.

2. In a small bowl, mix together the butter, garlic, red pepper flakes, lemon zest, half the parsley, and a pinch each of salt and pepper.

3. Arrange the butterflied shrimp tails in a single layer on the prepared baking sheet. Season with salt and pepper, and evenly divide the butter mixture in the center of each shrimp. Equally divide the bacon into spoonfuls and place on top of the butter.

4. Broil for 5 to 6 minutes, or until the shrimp are opaque and sizzling. Remove from the heat and transfer to a warmed platter. Drizzle the lemon juice over the shrimp and top with the remaining half of the parsley. Serve immediately with crusty bread.

PREPARATION TIP: To butterfly the shrimp, start from the head and insert the tip of a paring knife three-quarters of the way into the shrimp. Do not cut all the way through the shrimp. Make a slice down the center of the shrimp's back from the head area to the tail, but do not cut into the tail area. Open the shrimp like a book and spread it flat. Wipe away the vein (the shrimp's digestive tract, if it is visible) and rinse under cold water, then blot dry with a paper towel.

PER SERVING: Calories: 602; Total fat: 44g; Protein: 49g; Carbohydrates: 3g; Fiber: <1g; Sugar: <1g; Sodium: 1,414mg

CHILEAN SEA BASS WITH ROASTED LEMONS AND FRESH HERBS

GLUTEN-FREE / DAIRY-FREE / NUT-FREE
SERVES 4 / PREP TIME: 10 MINUTES / COOK TIME: 25 MINUTES

This is the simplest way to prepare fish for dinner—especially a fish like Chilean sea bass, which is so rich and buttery it doesn't need much accompaniment. We caramelize the lemons slightly and add some tomatoes for color and brightness.

2 lemons, sliced ¼ to ⅛ inch thick

4 tablespoons extra-virgin olive oil, divided

Kosher salt

Freshly ground black pepper

4 (6-ounce) Chilean sea bass fillets

Pinch red pepper flakes

1 tablespoon roughly chopped fresh oregano

2 teaspoons roughly chopped fresh rosemary

2 tablespoons roughly chopped flat leaf parsley

½ cup grape tomatoes, sliced in half

1. Heat the oven to 425°F.

2. Toss the lemons with 2 tablespoons of olive oil in a bowl and spread them out in an even layer on a baking sheet lined with parchment. Roast the lemons for 10 minutes, or until they look caramelized. Remove from the oven and set aside.

3. Place the fish in a baking dish and season on both sides with salt and pepper. In a small bowl, toss together the remaining 2 tablespoons of olive oil, the red pepper flakes, the oregano, the rosemary, and the parsley, and spoon the mixture onto the fish. Top with the roasted lemon slices and scatter the tomatoes around the dish.

4. Bake for 10 to 12 minutes, or until the fish is opaque. The fish should flake lightly when pushed gently with a fork. Transfer to warmed plates and evenly divide the lemons and tomatoes on top. Serve hot.

PREPARATION TIP: Save a step and lay the lemon slices down on top of the fish. Roast the fish, then flash-broil it for a few seconds until the lemons begin to brown and caramelize.

PER SERVING: Calories: 544; Total fat: 19g; Protein: 22g; Carbohydrates: 11g; Fiber: 3g; Sugar: 1g; Sodium: 200mg

SEAFOOD PAELLA

GLUTEN-FREE / DAIRY-FREE / NUT-FREE
SERVES 4 TO 6 / PREP TIME: 30 MINUTES / COOK TIME: 1 HOUR

The story goes that paella is derived from *para ella*, ("for her" in Spanish) when Sunday dinner was cooked by the men in the family so the mothers could rest. Even if it's not true, I love the idea, and in my cooking classes I encourage families to make this for Mother's Day. A bonus of paella is the caramelized layer of rice, called the "socorrat," that forms on the bottom of the pan during cooking. This crispy treat is one of my favorite parts of the paella.

3 to 4 cups fish or shrimp broth

1 small pinch saffron threads

**¼ cup olive oil, plus
  2 tablespoons**

1 medium onion, grated

2 large Roma tomatoes, grated

4 garlic cloves, minced

Kosher salt

Freshly ground black pepper

1 tablespoon water, if needed

**1½ cups medium-grain white
  rice, rinsed**

1 teaspoon smoked paprika

¼ teaspoon cayenne pepper

**12 uncooked extra-large shrimp
  (26–30 shrimp per pound),
  peeled and deveined**

**1 pound monkfish or halibut
  fillets, skinned and deboned,
  and cut into 1-inch chunks**

**12 fresh littleneck clams,
  scrubbed**

**12 fresh mussels, scrubbed,
  beards removed**

1 cup frozen peas

2 tablespoons chopped parsley

2 lemons, cut into 6 to 8 wedges

1. Pick through the clams and mussels, tapping any open shells lightly against the counter. If the shells do not close up in response, they are not fresh and should be discarded.

2. Bring the fish broth to a simmer in a large saucepan over low heat. Crushing the saffron between your fingers, add it to the pan. The broth will turn golden yellow as the saffron steeps.

3. Heat a large 12- to 14-inch paella pan over medium heat and add ¼ cup of olive oil. Add the onion, tomatoes, and garlic with a pinch of salt and pepper and cook until the mixture turns dark red and jammy, about 10 to 15 minutes. This mixture is called "sofrito." If any sticks to the pan, add 1 tablespoon of water to deglaze and scrape it off.

4. Push the sofrito to the edges of the pan and add the 2 tablespoons of olive oil in the center of the pan. Add the rice and stir the rice and oil for 2 to 3 minutes until the rice is toasted and turns white in the center of the grain. Stir together with the sofrito and add the paprika and cayenne.

5. Pour in the hot broth, reserving 1 cup. Stir to dislodge any bits that may be stuck to the bottom of the pan. Turn the heat to low and scrape down any rice stuck to the sides. Gently simmer for 18 to 20 minutes, uncovered. Monitor the pan occasionally, rotating it to make sure it heats evenly as the rice cooks.

6. When the rice is nearly cooked, it will push up through the stock. At this point, add the shrimp, fish, clams, and mussels, and gently push them down into the rice. Scatter the peas over the top. Cover the pan with foil and cook on low heat until the shellfish open and the shrimp turn opaque and pink, another 5 to 7 minutes. Test one grain of rice for doneness—it should be chewy without any hint of chalkiness when you bite into it. If the rice needs to continue cooking, drizzle a little more broth over the paella and cook for another 5 to 8 minutes, covered.

7. Remove from the heat and let the paella rest for 10 minutes. Remove any clams or mussels that have not opened—they are dead and should be discarded. Sprinkle the parsley and squeeze the lemon juice over the entire pan, and serve hot.

PREPARATION TIP: Sofrito is the flavor base of this dish. I make twice the amount needed and freeze the extra. If the craving for paella strikes, I'm halfway there!

INGREDIENT TIP: Use the largest holes on a box grater to grate the onion and tomato. The tomato will become pulpy, which is what you want.

PER SERVING: Calories: 777; Total fat: 27g; Protein: 57g; Carbohydrates: 80g; Fiber: 7g; Sugar: 7g; Sodium: 718mg

SPAGHETTI WITH CLAMS

NUT-FREE
SERVES 4 TO 6 / PREP TIME: 20 MINUTES / COOK TIME: 30 MINUTES

This is a twist on my favorite pasta dish, using chewy spaghetti and adding a crunchy texture with lemony bread crumbs. This is a great recipe to cook in a wok if you have one—its shape is perfect for tossing pasta and sauce together.

6 cloves of garlic, finely minced, divided

3 tablespoons roughly chopped flat leaf parsley, divided

1½ cups panko bread crumbs

2 oil-packed anchovy fillets, finely chopped, oil reserved

Zest of 1 lemon

3 tablespoons kosher salt, plus additional for seasoning

2 gallons water

12 ounces dried spaghetti

3 tablespoons extra-virgin olive oil

1 large shallot, thinly sliced

Generous pinch red pepper flakes

½ cup dry white wine, such as Pinot Grigio

3 pounds littleneck clams, scrubbed thoroughly under cold running water

3 tablespoons unsalted butter, at room temperature

Juice of 1 lemon

1. In a small bowl, mix 1 teaspoon of garlic, 1 tablespoon of parsley, and the bread crumbs. Drizzle in 1 or 2 teaspoons of the reserved anchovy oil and mix together. In a small skillet, toast the bread crumbs mixture on medium heat until golden brown. Stir in the lemon zest, season with a pinch of salt, and set aside.

2. In a large stockpot, bring the water to a boil over high heat and add 3 tablespoons of salt. Cook the spaghetti according to package instructions.

3. Meanwhile, add the olive oil to a large sauté pan or wok over medium-high heat. Sauté the shallot and anchovies until soft, 3 to 4 minutes. Add the remaining garlic and the red pepper flakes and sauté until the garlic is fragrant, about 1 minute more.

4. Lower the heat to medium. Add the wine and simmer while you pick through the clams, discarding any that are still open. Toss in the clams and cover the pan. The steam will cook the clams in 8 to 10 minutes, and the clams will open once they're done. When the majority of the clams have opened, discard any that are still closed.

5. Drain the pasta, setting aside 1 cup of the cooking liquid. In the sauté pan, toss the pasta and clams together with the butter. Drizzle a generous amount of lemon juice over the pasta. If the sauce looks a little dry, add a small amount of the pasta water. Sprinkle the bread crumbs over the top and serve immediately.

PREPARATION TIP: In the time it takes for the water to boil and the pasta to cook, the sauce should be ready. Canned clams are a great substitute for fresh in this recipe, so keep a 14-ounce can of them on hand for those nights you want a quick and easy dinner.

PER SERVING: Calories: 1,176; Total fat: 30g; Protein: 107g; Carbohydrates: 112g; Fiber: 3g; Sugar: 5g; Sodium: 6,484mg

LOWCOUNTRY BOIL

GLUTEN-FREE / NUT-FREE / ONE POT
SERVES 12 / PREP TIME: 20 MINUTES / COOK TIME: 20 MINUTES

This Lowcountry Boil comes from South Carolina and is a great (and delicious) way to feed a crowd. It is typically cooked and enjoyed outdoors: The ingredients are boiled, then spread out over newspapers directly on the table for folks to pull up to and enjoy together.

4 pounds small red potatoes, scrubbed

2 smoked ham hocks

1 (3-ounce) bag crab boil seasoning, such as Zatarain's

3 tablespoons Old Bay seasoning

5 quarts water

3 medium sweet onions, cut into 6 wedges each

2 pounds kielbasa or hot-smoked link sausage, sliced into 1½-inch pieces

6 ears of corn, halved

4 pounds extra-large shrimp (26–30 shrimp per pound), peeled and deveined

4 to 6 lemons, cut into 6 wedges each

Cocktail sauce, for serving

Melted butter, for serving

1. To a large stockpot, add the potatoes, ham hocks, and crab boil seasoning, and cover with the water. Cover the pot, bring to a rolling boil on high heat, and cook for 5 minutes.

2. Add the onions, sausage, and corn, and return to a boil. Cook for 10 minutes, or until the potatoes are tender.

3. Add the Old Bay seasoning and the shrimp and cook for 3 to 4 minutes, or until the shrimp turn pink and opaque. Lift the solid ingredients from the stockpot using a wire mesh skimmer and transfer to two or three large serving platters. Arrange the lemon wedges around the piles of seafood, and serve with bowls of cocktail sauce and melted butter on the side.

SERVING TIP: Though not traditional, a fresh green herb salad and slabs of garlic bread are terrific accompaniments to this dish.

PER SERVING: Calories: 617; Total fat: 28g; Protein: 51g; Carbohydrates: 45g; Fiber: 8g; Sugar: 5g; Sodium: 1,570mg

CAJUN CATFISH AND SPINACH STEW

DAIRY-FREE / NUT-FREE / ONE POT
SERVES 4 / PREP TIME: 15 MINUTES / COOK TIME: 40 MINUTES

In Cajun cooking, the combination of onion, celery, and bell pepper is known as the "holy trinity." Similar to the French mirepoix trio of carrot, onion, and celery, the holy trinity gives an authentic Cajun flavor to whatever recipe it's used in. I add kidney beans and bacon to this stew in a nod to another famous Cajun recipe—red beans and rice.

½ pound thick-cut bacon, cut into ½-inch pieces

1 small onion, cut into ¼-inch cubes

2 stalks celery, cut into ¼-inch cubes

1 medium green bell pepper, cored and cut into ¼-inch cubes

Kosher salt

Freshly ground black pepper

1 (14-ounce) can kidney beans, drained and rinsed

2 tablespoons tomato paste

1 (14-ounce) can fire-roasted diced tomatoes

1 tablespoon Worcestershire sauce

½ teaspoon dried thyme

1½ cups chicken or fish broth

2 large Yukon Gold potatoes, peeled and diced

3 or 4 catfish fillets, cut into 1½-inch chunks

3 cups roughly chopped spinach leaves and stems

Louisiana hot sauce, such as Frank's RedHot, for serving

1. In a large Dutch oven over medium-high heat, cook the bacon until brown and crispy, 5 to 6 minutes. Add the onion, celery, and bell pepper, and sauté in the bacon fat until tender and the onions are translucent, about 7 minutes. Season with salt and pepper. Add the kidney beans and tomato paste. Continue to cook, stirring occasionally, for another 2 minutes.

2. Add the tomatoes, Worcestershire sauce, thyme, and broth. Stir to combine. Add the potatoes and bring to a boil, about 5 minutes. Lower the heat to medium-low and simmer for another 5 minutes. Add the catfish and simmer for 10 minutes, or until the catfish is flaky and the potatoes are soft. Taste and season with salt and pepper, if needed.

3. Turn off the heat and let the stew rest for 5 minutes. Stir in the chopped spinach and let the spinach wilt. To serve, spoon the stew into warmed bowls and serve hot with a side of hot sauce.

INGREDIENT TIP: Avoid using baby spinach, which is too tender. Mature spinach will keep its shape and give bright spots of green to the stew.

SUBSTITUTION TIP: This stew is fantastic with 1 pound of either tilapia or shrimp instead of catfish.

PER SERVING: Calories: 715; Total fat: 39g; Protein: 37g; Carbohydrates: 58g; Fiber: 11g; Sugar: 7g; Sodium: 1,289mg

TUNA NOODLE CASSEROLE

NUT-FREE

SERVES 6 TO 8 / PREP TIME: 15 MINUTES / COOK TIME: 50 MINUTES

This is an upscale, scratch-made version of the traditional favorite that uses canned condensed mushroom soup. Full of fresh vegetables with a velvety sauce, it's a little more work, but it's worth the effort!

1 gallon water

3 tablespoons kosher salt, plus additional as needed

¾ pound extra-wide dried egg noodles

6 tablespoons unsalted butter, melted, divided

1½ cups white mushrooms, cleaned and cut into ¼-inch-thick slices

½ small yellow onion, chopped

2 stalks celery, cut into ¼-inch cubes

2 tablespoons dry sherry

Pinch cayenne pepper

4 tablespoons all-purpose flour

¾ cup half and half

¾ cup fish broth

2 (4-ounce) cans solid tuna, packed in oil, drained and oil reserved

2 tablespoons finely chopped flat leaf parsley

½ cup panko bread crumbs

1. Preheat the oven to 350°F. Bring the water to boil in a medium stockpot. Add 3 tablespoons of salt and cook the noodles according to package instructions. While the noodles are cooking, brush 2 tablespoons of melted butter all over the inside of a 9-by-13-inch baking dish. Set aside. Drain the noodles and return to the pot when finished. Set aside.

2. In a large sauté pan over medium-high heat, sauté the mushrooms with the remaining 4 tablespoons of butter. Add a pinch of salt and sauté until golden brown, about 8 minutes. Add the onion and celery, and sauté for 4 minutes more.

3. Lower the heat to medium-low and add the sherry. Stir briefly and cook until the sherry has evaporated. Season with another pinch of salt and the cayenne. Sprinkle in the flour and stir until the vegetables are coated.

4. Add the half and half and broth, and keep stirring until the sauce thickens, 2 to 3 minutes. Turn off the heat and gently fold in the tuna and parsley until combined. Transfer the tuna mixture to the pot of cooked egg noodles and fold to combine, then pour the ingredients into the prepared baking dish.

5. In a small bowl, stir together 1 tablespoon of the reserved tuna oil with the bread crumbs and a pinch of salt. Sprinkle on top of the casserole.

6. Bake for 25 minutes, or until the casserole is bubbling and the bread crumb topping is golden brown. Remove from the oven and let rest for 10 minutes. Serve hot.

INGREDIENT TIP: Canned tuna packed in oil is more flavorful than the water-packed type. When draining the oil, don't squeeze the tuna bone-dry; leave a bit in the tuna. Use the drained oil in salad dressing or drizzled over pasta.

PER SERVING: Calories: 473; Total fat: 20g; Protein: 21g; Carbohydrates: 53g; Fiber: 2g; Sugar: 5g; Sodium: 4,978mg

FISH TACOS WITH PICKLED VEGETABLES

GLUTEN-FREE / NUT-FREE
SERVES 4 (2 TACOS EACH) / PREP TIME: 30 MINUTES / COOK TIME: 10 MINUTES

Anytime is the perfect time for fish tacos! Invite some friends over and make a double or triple batch of this recipe. These tacos are heart-healthy, fresh, and light, but very satisfying and flavorful. My friend Maria makes her own tortillas by hand, which makes these extra special.

FOR THE PICKLED VEGETABLES

½ cup sugar

¾ cup distilled white vinegar

1 teaspoon kosher salt

¾ cup water

½ cup shredded carrots

½ small red onion, thinly sliced

1 large jalapeño, seeded and sliced into thin strips

FOR THE TACOS

1 pound cod fillets (or any flaky white fish), cut into 4 pieces

Kosher salt

Freshly ground black pepper

½ teaspoon chili powder

1 teaspoon ground cumin

3 tablespoons vegetable oil

8 (6-inch) corn tortillas

1 lime, cut into 4 wedges

2 tablespoons sour cream (or Mexican crema)

¼ cup cilantro leaves, loosely packed

TO PICKLE THE VEGETABLES

1. In a small saucepan over medium-high heat, combine the sugar, vinegar, and salt with the water. Stir until the sugar dissolves, then bring the mixture to a boil. Turn off the heat and cool, about 10 minutes. Add the carrots, onion, and jalapeño, and steep for 20 minutes, or up to 2 hours.

TO MAKE THE TACOS

2. As the vegetables pickle, heat a cast iron skillet over medium-high heat. Season both sides of the fish with salt and pepper, the chili powder, and the cumin. Add the oil to the pan and wait until it begins to smoke slightly. Add the fish to the pan and sear for 4 minutes per side. Remove from the heat and place the fish on a clean plate, then tent with foil.

3. Wipe out the pan with a dry paper towel and return it to medium-high heat. Toast the tortillas, 2 at a time, for 30 seconds per side.

4. To assemble, break the fillets into smaller chunks and arrange them on top of the tortillas. Season each taco lightly with salt and pepper and a squeeze of lime juice. Top each with pickled vegetables, a drizzle of sour cream, and cilantro. Serve immediately.

PRO TIP: Speed up the pickling by adding the vegetables while the liquid is still hot, then set the bowl in an ice water bath. In the time it takes for the mixture to chill, the pickles will be done!

SERVING TIP: Add avocado slices for a creamy garnish, and sliced radishes for a crunchy bite.

PER SERVING: Calories: 454; Total fat: 15g; Protein: 29g; Carbohydrates: 54g; Fiber: 5g; Sugar: 23g; Sodium: 721mg

FRIED CALAMARI WITH RUSTIC TOMATO SAUCE

DAIRY-FREE / NUT-FREE / 30 MINUTE

SERVES 4 / PREP TIME: 10 MINUTES / COOK TIME: 20 MINUTES

There is a strong debate over which is the correct dipping sauce for fried calamari: On the East Coast it's a zesty marinara, while on the West Coast it's cocktail sauce. The dipping sauce in this recipe more closely resembles marinara, but whatever you serve it with, fried calamari at home is a real treat!

FOR THE DIPPING SAUCE

2 tablespoons extra-virgin olive oil

1 small shallot, finely minced

1 garlic clove, finely minced

Kosher salt

Freshly ground black pepper

1 (14-ounce) can tomato purée

1 bay leaf

1 teaspoon balsamic vinegar (optional)

FOR THE CALAMARI

1½ quarts vegetable oil

1½ cups all-purpose flour

1½ cups rice flour

1 tablespoon finely minced parsley

1 teaspoon freshly ground black pepper

Kosher salt

2 pounds squid with tentacles, bodies cut into ⅓- to ½-inch-thick rings

1 lemon, cut into 4 wedges

TO MAKE THE DIPPING SAUCE

1. Heat a medium saucepan over medium-high heat. Add the olive oil and sauté the shallot and garlic with a pinch each of salt and pepper. Cook until the shallots are soft and translucent, 4 to 5 minutes. Add the tomato purée and bay leaf and stir to combine. Lower the heat to medium-low. Simmer for 10 minutes and taste and add more salt if needed. Stir in the balsamic vinegar (if using). Set aside and keep warm.

TO MAKE THE CALAMARI

2. Heat the vegetable oil to 350°F in a Dutch oven over medium-high heat. In a large bowl, mix the all-purpose flour, the rice flour, the parsley, the pepper, and a pinch of salt. Working in small batches, blot the calamari with paper towels. Sprinkle with a pinch of salt and dredge in the flour mixture to coat. Use a wire skimmer or slotted spoon to lower the calamari into the oil. Fry until crisp and golden, 1 to 2 minutes. Skim the calamari out and place on a paper towel–lined plate. Season lightly with salt. Repeat with the remaining calamari.

3. Serve on a warm platter with the lemon wedges and the warm tomato sauce on the side.

PREPARATION TIP: Calamari cooks quickly but becomes rubbery if overcooked. Keep an eye on the heat and adjust up or down to keep the oil at a steady 350°F, frying until just crisp and golden.

VARIATION TIP: With the same flour mixture, you can dredge thin slices of jalapeños and onions and toss in with the fried calamari.

PER SERVING: Calories: 1,163; Total fat: 65g; Protein: 46g; Carbohydrates: 101g: Fiber: 6g; Sugar: 6g; Sodium: 557mg

SALMON TERIYAKI

DAIRY-FREE / NUT-FREE / ONE POT
SERVES 4 / PREP TIME: 20 MINUTES / COOK TIME: 15 MINUTES

Authentic salmon teriyaki is terrific over white rice or noodles. With just 4 ingredients for the glaze, this is the real deal. Double up the recipe for leftovers or to use with other dishes and freeze the rest so you always have a delicious teriyaki sauce on hand.

½ cup sake

¼ mirin

¼ cup soy sauce

½ teaspoon grated fresh ginger

4 (3-ounce) salmon fillets, skin on, pin bones removed

Kosher salt

Freshly ground black pepper

2 tablespoons vegetable oil or canola oil, plus more as needed

1 teaspoon toasted sesame seeds, for garnish

1 scallion, thinly sliced, for garnish

1. In a small bowl, whisk together the sake, mirin, soy sauce, and ginger. Set aside. Season the salmon on both sides with salt and pepper.

2. Heat a 10-inch nonstick skillet over medium-high heat and add the oil. When the oil looks shimmery, sear the salmon, skin-side down, for 6 minutes. Tilt the pan occasionally to redistribute the oil. Use a fish spatula to gently flip the fillet, cooking the other side for another 2 minutes. Add more oil, 1 teaspoon at a time, if needed to keep the fish from sticking to the pan.

3. Transfer the salmon to a plate and wipe the oil from the pan with a paper towel. Pour in the sauce mixture and boil at medium-high heat until it reduces by two-thirds, about 3 minutes.

4. Return the salmon to the pan, skin-side up, and spoon the sauce over the top. Keep cooking for another 2 minutes, or until the salmon is cooked through (a digital thermometer should read 125°F).

5. Transfer the salmon to warmed plates. Spoon the sauce over the top and garnish with the sesame seeds and scallions.

SUBSTITUTION TIP: Skewer some shrimp or scallops and sear or broil them. Brush the teriyaki sauce on, then broil or grill.

PER SERVING: Calories: 273; Total fat: 15g; Protein: 19g; Carbohydrates: 10g; Fiber: <1g; Sugar: 4g; Sodium: 1,071mg

SOLE MEUNIÈRE

NUT-FREE / 30 MINUTES / ONE POT
SERVES 4 / PREP TIME: 10 MINUTES / COOK TIME: 15 MINUTES

This classic dish was Julia Child's first meal in Paris! In the classic presentation, it is efficiently deboned tableside by a practiced waiter. At home, however, you can buy boneless fillets to make it easier on yourself.

4 sole fillets, skinned and deboned

Kosher salt

Freshly ground black pepper

⅔ cup all-purpose flour

2 tablespoons vegetable oil

1 stick unsalted butter, divided into 3 and 5 tablespoons and cut into ½-inch cubes

2 tablespoons roughly chopped flat leaf parsley

Juice of ½ lemon

1. Season the fish on both sides with salt and pepper. Pour the flour into a wide, shallow dish and dredge both sides of the fish in the flour.

2. Heat the oil in a large nonstick skillet over medium-high heat. When the oil becomes shimmery, add 3 tablespoons of butter and quickly swirl to combine. When the butter stops foaming, add the fish and cook for 3 minutes per side. Both sides should be golden brown. Transfer to a plate and tent with foil.

3. Pour off the oil from the pan and wipe clean with a paper towel. Return the pan back to medium-high heat and add the remaining 5 tablespoons of butter. Cook until the milk solids begin to brown, 3 to 4 minutes. Turn off the heat and gently stir in the parsley and lemon juice—taking care, as the sauce may splatter. Season with salt and pepper and spoon the sauce over the fish to serve.

SUBSTITUTION TIP: Switch it up and make this dish with salmon, or use trout and sliced almonds for trout amandine.

SERVING TIP: Though not traditional, a garnish of chopped fresh dill brightens up the dish.

PER SERVING: Calories: 430; Total fat: 32g; Protein: 23g; Carbohydrates: 15g; Fiber: 1g; Sugar: 0g; Sodium: 94mg

BLACKENED CATFISH

NUT-FREE / 30 MINUTE
SERVES 4 / PREP TIME: 15 MINUTES / COOK TIME: 15 MINUTES

Blackened is not burned! This fish is rubbed with a spice mixture, then seared in an extra-hot cast iron skillet, which gives the fish an extremely dark and crispy crust. The most important tip I can give you is to **cook this fish outdoors**—the smoke will set off every smoke detector in your house if you try to cook it on the stovetop.

FOR THE BLACKENING RUB

1 teaspoon dried oregano

1 teaspoon dried thyme

1 tablespoon paprika

1 teaspoon garlic powder

1 teaspoon onion powder

½ teaspoon cayenne pepper

1 teaspoon kosher salt

½ teaspoon freshly ground black pepper

FOR THE CATFISH

8 tablespoons (1 stick) unsalted butter, divided

4 catfish fillets, blotted dry

2 tablespoons vegetable oil

2 garlic cloves, peeled and smashed

1 lemon, cut into 8 slices

2 tablespoons chopped fresh rosemary

2 teaspoons Worcestershire sauce

¼ cup dry white wine, such as Sauvignon Blanc

TO MAKE THE BLACKENING RUB

1. Crush the oregano and thyme in your fingers and add them to a small bowl, then add the paprika, garlic powder, onion powder, cayenne, salt, and pepper.

TO MAKE THE CATFISH

2. On an outdoor gas grill, preheat a large cast iron skillet over high heat until very hot and smoking.

3. Meanwhile, melt 4 tablespoons (half a stick) of butter in a small pan. Use paper towels to blot the catfish dry, and brush the melted butter on both sides of the catfish. Coat both sides of the fish with the blackening rub.

4. When the cast iron skillet starts smoking, lower the heat to medium-high and add the vegetable oil and 2 tablespoons butter. As soon as the butter melts, swirl the pan to combine. Cook the fish for 2 minutes per side, flipping with a thin, flexible metal spatula. The fish will smoke immediately and the spices may form a dark crust, but hold your nerve! Transfer the fish to warmed plates and tent with foil to keep warm.

5. Lower the heat to medium-low and add the garlic, lemon slices, and rosemary. Sauté for 1 minute. Add the Worcestershire sauce and wine. Simmer to reduce the wine by half, about 5 minutes. Turn off the heat and add the remaining 2 tablespoons of butter, swirling until just melted. Spoon the sauce over each fillet and garnish with the caramelized lemon slices. Serve hot.

COOKING TIP: It bears repeating: This recipe must be cooked outdoors and with a cast iron skillet.

SERVING TIP: Blackened catfish can be fiery spicy! Serve with cooked rice tossed with lots of fresh herbs and lemon zest to neutralize the heat.

PER SERVING: Calories: 397; Total fat: 32g; Protein: 21g; Carbohydrates: 7g; Fiber: 3g; Sugar: 1g; Sodium: 694mg

STEAMED MUSSELS WITH WHITE WINE AND FENNEL

NUT-FREE / 30 MINUTE / ONE POT
SERVES 4 / PREP TIME: 10 MINUTES / COOK TIME: 15 MINUTES

Mussels are quick to cook and relatively inexpensive. Stop at the grocery store on your way home and pick up a few pounds of them (and a nice crusty French baguette to serve with them). In less than 30 minutes, congratulate yourself on making a splendid meal!

4 pounds mussels, cleaned

4 tablespoons unsalted butter

1 small fennel bulb, halved and thinly sliced

2 small shallots, thinly sliced

4 large garlic cloves, thinly sliced

Kosher salt

Freshly ground black pepper

Pinch red pepper flakes

½ cup dry white wine, such as Sauvignon Blanc

¼ cup roughly chopped flat leaf parsley

1 crusty French baguette

1. Debeard the mussels by pulling off any fibrous clumps hanging from the shells, using your fingers or a pair of tweezers.

2. In a large Dutch oven over medium heat, melt the butter. Add the fennel, shallots, and garlic, and season with salt and pepper. Sauté until the shallots and garlic are translucent, 2 to 3 minutes. Do not let them brown. Add the red pepper flakes and cook for another 1 minute.

3. Add the wine and bring to a boil on high heat, then add the mussels to the pot. Lower the heat to medium-low, then cover and steam for 6 to 7 minutes, until the mussels open, lifting the lid halfway during cooking to give them a stir.

4. Remove from the heat and discard any mussels that are still closed. Toss in the parsley. Serve with crusty bread for dipping in the sauce.

SUBSTITUTION TIP: If you can find them, the green-lipped mussels from New Zealand are beautiful in a Thai version of this recipe using 2 stalks of minced lemongrass, a pinch of curry powder, and 1 (14-ounce) can coconut milk.

PER SERVING: Calories: 930; Total fat: 32g; Protein: 109g; Carbohydrates: 40g; Fiber: 2g; Sugar: 1g; Sodium: 1,710mg

SCALLOP AND CLAM PAN ROAST

NUT-FREE / ONE POT
SERVES 4 / PREP TIME: 15 MINUTES / COOK TIME: 25 MINUTES

New York's landmark Grand Central Oyster Bar on the lower level of Grand Central Terminal is a destination for all seafood lovers. My favorite dish that they serve there, the pan roast, is not quite a soup, not really a stew, but a wonderfully flavored seafood sauce ladled over a sponge of white bread. Here is my version. I hope you like it!

12 fresh sea scallops

Kosher salt

4 tablespoons unsalted butter

12 littleneck or cherrystone clams, shucked

1 celery stalk, thinly sliced

½ cup bottled clam juice

2 teaspoons Heinz Chili Sauce

1 teaspoon Worcestershire sauce

1 cup half and half

4 slices white bread, lightly toasted and each cut into 4 triangles

4 teaspoons smoked paprika

Chopped fresh parsley, for garnish (optional)

1. Blot the scallops dry with a paper towel and lightly season on both sides with salt. In a wide, shallow sauté pan, melt the butter over medium heat. When the butter stops foaming, add the scallops in a clockwise pattern, starting at 12 o'clock, so they cook for the same amount of time before you flip them. Sear the scallops for 5 to 6 minutes per side, or until they develop a lovely golden crust. Transfer to a warm plate and tent with foil.

2. Lower the heat to medium-low and add the clams and celery. Sauté lightly for 3 minutes, or until the celery turns translucent. Stir in the clam juice, chili sauce, Worcestershire sauce, and half and half. Simmer gently for 6 to 8 minutes, or until the clams open. Do not let the sauce boil, or it will curdle. Discard any clams that remain closed.

3. Lay the toast points into wide, shallow soup dishes and evenly divide the scallops and clams over the toasts. Spoon the sauce over the toasts and sprinkle with paprika. Garnish with chopped parsley (if using).

COOKING TIP: The key here is to gently simmer the sauce to let the flavors mingle and to avoid curdling when the half and half is added.

SUBSTITUTION TIP: You can make the classic Grand Central Oyster Bar pan roast with just oysters if you prefer.

PER SERVING: Calories: 438; Total fat: 22g; Protein: 28g; Carbohydrates: 32g; Fiber: 2g; Sugar: 10g; Sodium: 466mg

SEARED SCALLOPS WITH PINEAPPLE BEURRE BLANC

GLUTEN-FREE / NUT-FREE

SERVES 4 / PREP TIME: 10 MINUTES / COOK TIME: 30 MINUTES

In culinary school, I got the impression this was an important sauce after our chef reviewed the technique twice to make sure we got it. Over the years, I've settled on this pineapple version for scallops. It's well balanced and brings out the natural buttery sweetness of the scallops.

FOR THE BEURRE BLANC SAUCE

1 large shallot, finely minced

½ cup white wine vinegar

½ cup pineapple juice

½ cup white wine, such as Sauvignon Blanc

1 pound unsalted butter, cut into ½-inch cubes and chilled

FOR THE SCALLOPS

12 jumbo scallops (under 15 scallops per pound)

Kosher salt

Freshly ground black pepper

3 tablespoons ghee or clarified butter

Ice water, if needed

2 tablespoons thinly sliced fresh chives

TO MAKE THE BEURRE BLANC SAUCE

1. In a medium skillet, combine the shallot, vinegar, pineapple juice, and white wine. Bring to a boil on high heat, then lower to medium. Simmer for 15 to 20 minutes, or until the liquid has reduced to about 2 tablespoons.

2. Increase the heat to medium-high. Remove the butter from the refrigerator and add a few cubes at a time, whisking vigorously. As the butter melts, it should take on a velvety texture while being whisked. When you have 3 or 4 pieces of butter remaining, take the pan off the heat and stir in the last pieces until incorporated. Set aside and keep warm, but not hot.

TO MAKE THE SCALLOPS

3. Heat a cast iron skillet over medium-high heat. Blot the scallops dry with a paper towel and season both sides with salt and pepper. As soon as the skillet starts to smoke, add the ghee and swirl quickly to coat the pan.

4. Add the scallops to the pan in a clockwise pattern, starting at 12 o'clock so they cook for the same amount of time before you flip them. Sear for 3 minutes per side, or until they develop a good deep-seared crust. Transfer the scallops to a plate and tent with foil.

5. Reheat the beurre blanc sauce over medium-high heat, whisking vigorously until warm again. Do not overheat, or the sauce will separate. If that happens, don't panic. Quickly whisk in ice water, 1 tablespoon at a time, until the sauce comes back together.

6. Plate by spooning generous amounts of sauce on the bottoms of warmed serving plates, and arrange 3 scallops per plate. Garnish with the chives and serve hot.

INGREDIENT TIP: Beurre blanc is a delicate emulsion of melted butter and concentrated vinegar and wine. Classic preparations strain out the shallots after reducing, but I quite like the little bits for texture.

VARIATION TIP: Use this sauce with any pan-seared or broiled fish. A classic beurre blanc reduces white wine vinegar and white wine, but feel free to play around with different vinegars, wines, and fruit juices to create your own signature sauce.

PER SERVING: Calories: 1,035; Total fat: 104g; Protein: 16g; Carbohydrates: 9g; Fiber: <1g; Sugar: 4g; Sodium: 215mg

THAI-SPICED SALMON FILLET EN PAPILLOTE

GLUTEN-FREE / DAIRY-FREE / NUT-FREE / ONE POT
SERVES 2 / PREP TIME: 30 MINUTES / COOK TIME: 15 MINUTES

Cooking *en papillote* (on pap-ee-YOAT) is French for cooking in a parchment-paper pouch. It sounds fancy and complicated, but it's actually very easy. The trick is to get the edges of the parchment sealed tightly to create an airtight environment in which the fish can roast and steam.

1 small shallot, thinly sliced

1 tablespoon grated fresh ginger

1 large lemongrass stalk, peeled and center core smashed and roughly chopped

¼ cup julienned or shredded carrots

1 small Thai chile, thinly sliced

Zest of 1 lime

3 tablespoons coconut oil, divided

2 (3-ounce) salmon fillets, skin on and pin bones removed

Kosher salt

Juice of 1 lime

2 tablespoons roughly chopped cilantro

1. Preheat the oven to 425°F.

2. In a small bowl, toss the shallot, ginger, lemongrass, carrots, chile, and lime zest together with 1 tablespoon of coconut oil and set aside.

3. Take a sheet of 12-by-18-inch parchment paper, fold it in half, and draw a half-heart shape starting at the inside of the fold. Using kitchen scissors, cut along the edges to create the heart shape. (If you don't have kitchen scissors, regular scissors will work; just make sure they're clean!)

4. Open the heart and place 1 salmon fillet in the center of one side of the heart. Lightly season the salmon with salt and drizzle with 1 tablespoon of coconut oil. Place half the vegetables on top. Gently fold the other half of the parchment heart over so the edges line up.

5. Starting at the curved end of the heart, make one folded crease about ¼ inch from the edge. Continue to make successive folds along the edge of the package, making sure each new fold starts from the center of the previous one so the folds overlap, keeping the package airtight. Make sure each crease is flat and straight.

6. When you reach the pointed end, fold the paper up, then fold it back and tuck it underneath the package. Transfer the package to a baking sheet and drizzle half the remaining coconut oil over the top. Use your fingertips to spread the oil over the surface of the package—this will ensure proper heat delivery. Repeat the process with the other salmon fillet and remaining vegetables.

7. Bake for 10 to 12 minutes, or until the packages are browned and puffy.

8. Remove the packages from the oven and let them rest for 1 or 2 minutes. The packages will start to deflate. Carefully cut around the edges to open the packages. Transfer the salmon to a plate and spoon the vegetables and any sauce drippings from the package over the top. Drizzle the salmon with lime juice and garnish with the cilantro. Serve immediately.

SUBSTITUTION TIP: This recipe works well with any flaky whitefish instead of the salmon.

PREPARATION TIP: Prepare the parchment package ahead of time and leave it in the refrigerator for up to one day. When you're ready to cook, simply slide it into the preheated oven and extend your cook time by 5 minutes.

PER SERVING: Calories: 296; Total fat: 23g; Protein: 18g; Carbohydrates: 3g; Fiber: 1g; Sugar: 2g; Sodium: 141mg

OYSTERS ROCKEFELLER

NUT-FREE
SERVES 4 / PREP TIME: 30 MINUTES / COOK TIME: 20 MINUTES

Oysters Rockefeller started out as a variation of escargot, slathering garlic-parsley butter over shucked oysters and broiling them. In the late nineteenth century, the dish developed its own luxurious reputation after being named after the richest man in America at the time, John D. Rockefeller. Subsequently, it underwent a makeover that added spinach, bread crumbs, and bacon. I've stripped it down to make it more accessible and less fussy.

16 bluepoint oysters, scrubbed

10 ounces baby spinach, rinsed and roughly chopped

8 tablespoons (1 stick) unsalted butter at room temperature, divided

½ cup panko bread crumbs

2 tablespoons all-purpose flour

Pinch nutmeg

Pinch cayenne pepper

1½ cups half and half

Kosher salt

Freshly ground black pepper

2 tablespoons finely minced flat leaf parsley

6 garlic cloves, finely minced

1. Preheat the oven to 450°F.

2. Arrange the oysters in a single layer on a baking sheet or baking dish lined with foil and set aside until the oven is at temperature. Bake the oysters for 6 to 7 minutes, or until they just begin to open their shells. Remove from the oven and set aside to cool. Lower the oven temperature to 400°F.

3. Wilt the spinach in a medium nonstick skillet over medium heat. Transfer to a strainer and squeeze the excess liquid out by pressing the spinach down with the back of a wooden spoon. Set the spinach aside.

4. Return the pan to medium-high heat and melt 4 tablespoons of butter. When the butter stops foaming, remove 2 tablespoons of it and stir into the bread crumbs, then set aside. Whisk the remaining butter in the pan with the flour, nutmeg, and cayenne pepper. When a paste has formed, add the half and half and keep whisking until it's smooth, lump-free, and starting to thicken. Season with a pinch each of salt and pepper. Stir in the spinach, then set aside.

5. In a small bowl, mix the remaining 4 tablespoons of butter with the parsley, garlic, and a generous pinch of salt. Chill in the refrigerator until ready to use.

6. Shuck the oysters. Hold one over a small bowl and remove the flat top shell. Use a spoon to separate the oyster from the bottom shell, catching any liquid from the oyster in the bowl. Leave the oyster in its bottom shell and return to the baking sheet. Repeat with the remaining oysters. Strain the oyster liquid into the spinach mixture and stir to combine.

7. Move the top oven rack down one level. Assemble the oysters by dividing the compound butter over each, then dividing the spinach mixture, then topping with the bread crumbs. Cup your palm and press down gently to compact the toppings on the oysters.

8. Bake the oysters at 400°F for 8 to 10 minutes, or until bubbling. Switch the oven to broil and broil for 2 minutes, or until the bread crumbs are golden and crispy. Serve immediately.

INGREDIENT TIP: Play around with the aromatics in the butter, adding chopped chiles, ginger, or perhaps 1 teaspoon of curry powder—these oysters can handle it!

PER SERVING: Calories: 439; Total fat: 35g; Protein: 14g; Carbohydrates: 22g; Fiber: 2g; Sugar: 4g; Sodium: 238mg

MACADAMIA-CRUSTED MAHI-MAHI

30 MINUTE / ONE POT
SERVES 4 / PREP TIME: 15 MINUTES / COOK TIME: 15 MINUTES

Mahi-mahi is a firm white-fleshed fish that pairs beautifully with nuts and tropical fruits. In terms of sustainability, Seafood Watch classifies line- or pole-caught mahi-mahi as a good choice. Avoid long-line harvesting, which is harmful to birds, sea turtles, and other marine life.

4 (5 to 6 ounce) mahi-mahi fillets, skinned and deboned

Kosher salt

Freshly ground black pepper

1 cup all-purpose flour

¼ teaspoon paprika (hot paprika optional)

2 eggs, beaten

1 cup macadamia nuts, finely chopped

1 cup panko bread crumbs

2 tablespoons unsalted butter

1 tablespoon vegetable oil

1 lime, cut into 4 wedges

1. To prepare the fish, season both sides with salt and pepper. Stir the flour and paprika together on a wide plate. Put the beaten eggs in a wide, shallow bowl. In another bowl, mix the macadamia nuts and the bread crumbs.

2. Heat a large nonstick skillet over medium-high heat and add the butter and oil, swirling them together as the butter melts.

3. While the butter and oil are heating, dip one fillet into the flour, coating the fish evenly. Shake off the excess flour and dip the fillet into the egg, then coat with the nuts and breadcrumb mixture. Repeat the process with the remaining fish.

4. Lower the fish into the skillet carefully to avoid backsplash. Cook for 4 to 6 minutes per side, or until golden brown. The fish is properly cooked when it flakes slightly when pushed with a fork. Using an instant-read thermometer, the internal temperature should reach 145°F. Transfer to a warmed plate and squeeze lime juice over each. Serve hot.

SERVING TIP: I like to serve this with coconut rice and lots of lime juice.

SUBSTITUTION TIP: Swap out the macadamia nuts for chopped almonds, pistachios, or shredded unsweetened coconut.

PER SERVING: Calories: 763; Total fat: 43g; Protein: 51g; Carbohydrates: 49g; Fiber: 5g; Sugar: 3g; Sodium: 293mg

ROASTED SALMON WITH LEMON-GARLIC BUTTER

GLUTEN-FREE / NUT-FREE / ONE POT
SERVES 4 / PREP TIME: 30 MINUTES / COOK TIME: 12 MINUTES

I'll be honest: This is my go-to fish recipe. I keep salmon fillets and all kinds of leftover compound butters in my freezer. I pull them out before I leave for work to thaw in the refrigerator during the day. Then, when I get home, making dinner is a snap!

FOR THE COMPOUND BUTTER

- **4 tablespoons unsalted butter (½ stick), at room temperature**
- **½ teaspoon kosher salt**
- **¼ teaspoon freshly ground black pepper**
- **2 garlic cloves, minced**
- **2 teaspoons lemon zest**
- **Pinch red pepper flakes**
- **2 teaspoons finely minced flat leaf parsley**

FOR THE SALMON

- **4 (5-ounce) salmon fillets, skin on, deboned**
- **1 tablespoon extra-virgin olive oil**
- **Kosher salt**
- **Freshly ground black pepper**
- **1 tablespoon finely minced flat leaf parsley**

TO MAKE THE COMPOUND BUTTER

1. In a small bowl, mix together the butter, salt, pepper, garlic, lemon zest, red pepper flakes, and parsley until combined. Set aside.

TO MAKE THE SALMON

2. Preheat the oven to 400°F.

3. Place the salmon in an 8-by-8-inch baking dish and drizzle with the olive oil on all sides. Season with salt and pepper and set aside to come to room temperature, about 20 minutes. This will ensure a more evenly cooked salmon.

4. Roast the salmon for 8 to 12 minutes. Remove from the oven; while still hot, top with 2 tablespoons of compound butter. The butter will melt, creating a simple but delicious sauce. Sprinkle the remaining parsley over the top and serve hot.

PREPARATION TIP: You will have compound butter left over from this recipe. Keep it in the freezer so you'll have some to add to whatever you're making at any time.

VARIATION TIP: Create an Asian-inspired compound butter with 1 teaspoon of miso paste and ½ teaspoon each of grated ginger, minced scallions, and soy sauce.

PER SERVING: Calories: 310; Total fat: 21g; Protein: 29g; Carbohydrates: 1g; Fiber: <1g; Sugar: <1g; Sodium: 382mg

FRIED SARDINES WITH GREMOLATA

DAIRY-FREE / NUT-FREE / 30 MINUTE / ONE POT
SERVES 4 / PREP TIME: 10 MINUTES / COOK TIME: 10 MINUTES

Gremolata is an Italian condiment made from chopped herbs, lemon zest, and garlic. It's a bright, fresh accent for just about any meat or fish. We use it here with fried sardines, though you could sprinkle it over roasted sardines, too.

FOR THE GREMOLATA

1 bunch flat leaf parsley leaves, washed and spun dry

2 garlic cloves, finely minced

Zest of 1 lemon

FOR THE SARDINES

1½ cups vegetable oil

1¼ cups rice flour

2½ teaspoons kosher salt, plus a pinch

¼ teaspoon cayenne pepper

1½ pounds fresh sardines, about 6 to 8, butterflied and deboned

¾ cup sparkling water, chilled, plus more if needed

TO MAKE THE GREMOLATA

1. Finely mince the parsley and transfer it to a clean, dry kitchen towel or cheesecloth. Gather it up into a tight knob and squeeze out the extra moisture. Transfer to a small mixing bowl and stir in the garlic and lemon zest.

TO MAKE THE SARDINES

2. Heat the oil to 375°F in a wide, shallow sauté pan over medium-high heat. While the oil is coming to temperature, combine the rice flour, 2½ teaspoons salt, and cayenne in a medium bowl. Blot the sardines on both sides with a paper towel and dredge them in the rice flour mixture. Transfer to a plate.

3. Whisk the sparkling water into the flour bowl. The batter should resemble thin pancake batter, so add more sparkling water, a splash at a time, if needed.

4. Check the oil temperature by dropping a teaspoon of batter into the pan. If it immediately sizzles and floats, the oil is ready. Dip the sardines one at a time into the batter and gently shake off the excess. Carefully lower away from you into the oil and fry until crispy and light golden brown, 6 to 7 minutes, flipping halfway through.

CONTINUED ▶

5. Use a slotted spoon or wire skimmer to transfer the sardines to a paper towel–lined platter to blot the excess oil. Season with a pinch of salt and serve on a warm platter with the gremolata sprinkled over the top.

PREPARATION TIP: Rinse out the green spot on your kitchen towel by rubbing it with coarse salt and cold water. The stain will come out in the wash with no problem—I promise!

INGREDIENT TIP: Buy the sardines already butterflied from the seafood counter and save yourself some time. Rice flour will yield a very light, crispy fried texture, but if you can't find it, you can always use all-purpose wheat flour. Similarly, keeping the sparkling water as cold as possible before mixing it into the batter will result in a lighter, crispier texture.

PER SERVING: Calories: 640; Total fat: 36g; Protein: 38g; Carbohydrates: 41g; Fiber: 2g; Sugar: <1g; Sodium: 1,462mg

BROILED HALIBUT WITH LEMON-HERB PERSILLADE

NUT-FREE / 30 MINUTE / ONE POT
SERVES 4 / PREP TIME: 10 MINUTES / COOK TIME: 15 MINUTES

Persillade (per-see-YAHD) is the French version of gremolata, giving any dish an herbal highlight. Halibut is a delicious mild and light whitefish with big flakes. It takes minutes to cook and is leaner than salmon. If you're looking for a lighter protein, go for the halibut!

FOR THE PERSILLADE

4 tablespoons unsalted butter, melted

Zest of 1 lemon

½ bunch flat leaf parsley, finely minced

2 tablespoons fresh oregano leaves, finely minced

2 teaspoons fresh thyme leaves, finely minced

¼ cup panko bread crumbs

Kosher salt

Freshly ground black pepper

FOR THE HALIBUT

1 lemon, cut into 8 thin slices

4 (5 to 6 ounce) halibut fillets

Kosher salt

Freshly ground black pepper

3 tablespoons unsalted butter, melted

TO MAKE THE PERSILLADE

1. In a small bowl, mix the butter, lemon zest, parsley, oregano, thyme, and bread crumbs, and season lightly with salt and pepper.

TO MAKE THE HALIBUT

2. Preheat the oven to 425°F. Line a baking sheet with foil or parchment paper.

3. On the baking sheet, make 4 beds of 2 lemon slices each for the halibut fillets. Place the fillets on top and season with salt and pepper.

4. Brush the melted butter over the tops and sides of the halibut, then roast for 8 to 12 minutes, or until the fish gently flakes when gently pressed with a fork.

5. Remove the pan from the oven and top each fillet generously with the persillade. Switch the oven to broil and broil the fish for 2 minutes, or until the bread crumbs are golden brown and toasted. Transfer to warmed plates and serve hot.

SUBSTITUTION TIP: Swap any flaky fish for the halibut. I like this dish with cod, haddock, sea bass, and salmon.

PER SERVING: Calories: 383; Total fat: 22g; Protein: 39g; Carbohydrates: 9g; Fiber: 2g; Sugar: <1g; Sodium: 116mg

GRILLED TUNA STEAKS WITH WASABI BUTTER

GLUTEN-FREE / NUT-FREE / 30 MINUTE / ONE POT
SERVES 4 / PREP TIME: 10 MINUTES / COOK TIME: 10 MINUTES

Compound butter makes another showstopping appearance in this recipe, this time with an Asian twist. Grilling the tuna briefly gives just enough heat to sear the outside but keeps the center nice and rare. If you cook the steaks all the way through, the fish will be dry and tough.

2 fresh tuna steaks, about 1 pound each

Kosher salt

Freshly ground black pepper

4 tablespoons (½ stick) unsalted butter, at room temperature

2 teaspoons wasabi paste

1 teaspoon rice vinegar

½ teaspoon sesame oil

2 tablespoons vegetable oil

Thinly sliced scallions, for garnish (optional)

1. Season the tuna steaks lightly on both sides with salt and pepper and set aside.

2. In a small bowl, mix together the butter, wasabi paste, rice vinegar, sesame oil, and a pinch of salt. Set aside.

3. Heat a grill pan over high heat until it begins to lightly smoke. Brush the tuna with the vegetable oil and sear for 2 minutes on each side. There should be dark grill marks on both sides. Transfer to a clean cutting board. Spread half the wasabi butter over each steak and tent with foil for 5 minutes.

4. Cut each steak into ½-inch slices across the grain and arrange on a warm platter. Spread any remaining butter over and serve warm. Garnish with thinly sliced scallions (if using).

INGREDIENT TIP: If you have powdered wasabi, mix it with a small amount of water to create a paste before adding it to the butter. In a pinch, save leftover wasabi from your sushi takeout!

PRO TIP: Buy the highest-quality tuna steaks that your budget allows. Because we are serving it so rare, it shouldn't be consumed by expectant mothers, young children, or anyone with a compromised immune system, just to be safe.

PER SERVING: Calories: 591; Total fat: 34g; Protein: 68g; Carbohydrates: 2g; Fiber: 0g; Sugar: 0g; Sodium: 165mg

COD IN SPICED TOMATO CURRY

GLUTEN-FREE / NUT-FREE / ONE POT
SERVES 4 / PREP TIME: 10 MINUTES / COOK TIME: 30 MINUTES

Indian food doesn't have to be complicated and time consuming. A quick recipe like this has all the satisfying flavors and aromas of Indian cuisine but with half the work. Cook the rice ahead of time, and this recipe comes together quickly and easily.

4 (5- to 6-ounce) cod fillets

Kosher salt

Freshly ground black pepper

4 tablespoons (½ stick) unsalted butter, or coconut oil

1 small yellow onion, cut into ¼-inch cubes

1 tablespoon (1½-inch piece) finely minced fresh ginger

3 cloves garlic, finely minced

2 tablespoons tomato paste

2 teaspoons Madras curry powder

¾ cup water

2 cups cooked basmati rice

Chopped cilantro, for garnish (optional)

1. Season the cod lightly with salt and pepper on all sides and set aside.

2. Heat the butter in a wide saucepan over medium heat. Add the onion, ginger, and garlic. Stir briefly, cover the pan, and sweat for 10 minutes, or until everything is soft and translucent. Season lightly with salt and pepper.

3. In a small bowl, stir together the tomato paste and curry powder with the water. Pour into the saucepan and stir to combine. Increase the heat to medium-high and simmer for about 5 minutes.

4. Reduce the heat to medium-low. Add the fish to the pan, cover, and simmer for 10 to 12 minutes. The fish will become opaque and should flake when pressed gently with a fork.

5. Evenly divide the rice among 4 warmed shallow bowls and top with the fish and sauce. Garnish with chopped cilantro (if using) and serve hot.

VARIATION TIP: Add a sliced potato to the sauce as it simmers to help bulk up the dish. The potato also helps thicken the sauce slightly.

PER SERVING: Calories: 374; Total fat: 13g; Protein: 35g; Carbohydrates: 27g; Fiber: 1g; Sugar: 2g; Sodium: 178mg

RED SNAPPER VERACRUZ

GLUTEN-FREE / DAIRY-FREE / NUT-FREE / ONE POT
SERVES 4 / PREP TIME: 15 MINUTES / COOK TIME: 40 MINUTES

This classic Mexican red snapper dish tastes better the next day, which is great because it's a slightly higher time investment. But it's worth it—and you can reap benefits later (hello, leftovers for lunch!). I've simplified it by simmering the snapper directly in the sauce instead of pan-frying the fish separately.

4 red snapper fillets

Kosher salt

Freshly ground black pepper

Juice of 2 limes, divided

2 tablespoons extra-virgin olive oil

1 medium yellow onion, cut into long, thin strips

1 large red bell pepper, cored and cut into ¼-inch-wide strips

3 garlic cloves, minced

1 teaspoon chili powder

1 teaspoon dried oregano

1 (14-ounce) can diced tomatoes

½ cup pitted green olives, roughly chopped

1 tablespoon capers, roughly chopped

1. Blot the fish with a paper towel and season with salt and pepper. Squeeze half the lime juice over the top and set aside.

2. Add the olive oil to a wide, shallow sauté pan over medium-high heat. When the oil starts to smoke, sauté the onion and bell pepper until the onion is soft and translucent, about 7 minutes. Season lightly with salt and pepper. Add the garlic, chili powder, and oregano, and continue to sauté for another 1 minute. Reduce the heat to medium and add the tomatoes, olives, and capers, and simmer for 8 to 10 minutes.

3. Add the fish to the sauce and cover. Simmer for 15 to 20 minutes, or until the fish is cooked; it should flake when gently pushed with a fork. Squeeze the remaining lime juice over the top and serve hot.

SERVING TIP: Serve this over Spanish rice or with warm tortillas. Garnish with chopped cilantro and pickled jalapeños.

SUBSTITUTION TIP: Tilapia, halibut, or cod are delicious in this dish if snapper is not available.

PER SERVING: Calories: 268; Total fat: 13g; Protein: 23g; Carbohydrates: 12g; Fiber: 3g; Sugar: 5g; Sodium: 586mg

PISTACHIO-CRUSTED TUNA AND LENTIL SALAD

DAIRY-FREE

SERVES 4 / PREP TIME: 15 MINUTES / COOK TIME: 35 MINUTES

Fish and lentils is a great match. This dish is protein-packed with nuts, tuna, and lentils. The recipe may seem complicated, but I promise you it's not. If time is tight, you can reach for the precooked lentils available in most supermarkets.

FOR THE LENTILS

1 cup Puy lentils

1 bay leaf

2 cups low-sodium vegetable broth

2 medium carrots, peeled and coarsely grated

2 scallions, thinly sliced

1 cup grape tomatoes, halved

Zest of 1 large lemon

Juice of 1 lemon

1 tablespoon red wine vinegar

1 tablespoon curry powder

½ cup extra-virgin olive oil

Kosher salt

Freshly ground black pepper

FOR THE TUNA

1 cup shelled pistachios

2 tablespoons all-purpose flour

4 (4- to 5-ounce) tuna steaks

Kosher salt

Freshly ground black pepper

2 tablespoons grapeseed oil or canola oil

TO MAKE THE LENTILS

1. In a medium saucepan over medium heat, add the lentils, bay leaf, and vegetable broth. Add water until the lentils are covered by 2 inches. Simmer over medium heat for 20 to 25 minutes, or until the lentils are tender but still firm. Drain, and discard the bay leaf. Transfer to a mixing bowl and set aside to cool.

2. Once the lentils have cooled slightly, fold in the carrots, scallions, tomatoes, and lemon zest. Stir in the lemon juice, vinegar, curry powder, and olive oil, and season with salt and pepper.

TO MAKE THE TUNA

3. Pulse the pistachios in a food processor until finely chopped. Transfer to a wide, shallow dish and stir in the flour. Season each side of the tuna with salt and pepper, then dredge the tuna in the pistachio mixture.

4. Heat the oil in a large nonstick skillet over medium-high heat. When the oil begins to smoke, sear the tuna for 7 to 8 minutes, flipping halfway through. Both sides should be brown and crispy, but the center should be medium-rare. The fish is done when an instant-read digital thermometer reads 130°F. Transfer to a warmed plate and tent with foil.

5. To serve, transfer the lentil salad to a warmed serving platter and top with the tuna steaks.

SUBSTITUTION TIP: Salmon makes a great alternative if tuna isn't available.

INGREDIENT TIP: Puy lentils are the dark green, smaller variety from France. If you can't find them, brown lentils will work; simply cook for a few minutes less to keep them firm, checking periodically for doneness.

PER SERVING: Calories: 842; Total fat: 55g; Protein: 50g; Carbohydrates: 39g; Fiber: 15g; Sugar: 6g; Sodium: 313mg

GRILLED SHRIMP KABOBS
WITH PESTO SAUCE

GLUTEN-FREE / 30 MINUTE

SERVES 4 / PREP TIME: 15 MINUTES / COOK TIME: 15 MINUTES

Colorful shrimp and vegetable kabobs drizzled with a bright green pesto sauce makes for a perfect summer grilling recipe. I added lemon to the pesto for acidity to brighten up the shrimp and add an extra pop of flavor. I like to serve these kabobs with grilled flatbread or on a bed of couscous.

FOR THE PESTO

1 packed cup fresh basil leaves

2 garlic cloves, smashed

¼ cup pine nuts, toasted

½ cup grated Parmesan cheese

Zest of 1 lemon

Juice of 1 lemon

½ cup extra-virgin olive oil

Kosher salt

Freshly ground black pepper

FOR THE SHRIMP KABOBS

8 cherry tomatoes

1 yellow summer squash, cut into roughly 8 (1-inch) chunks

1 zucchini, cut into roughly 8 (1-inch) chunks

1 red onion, cut into chunks

1½ pounds extra-jumbo shrimp (16–20 shrimp per pound), peeled and deveined

3 garlic cloves, finely minced

Pinch red pepper flakes

¼ cup extra-virgin olive oil

Kosher salt

TO MAKE THE PESTO

1. In a food processor or blender, blend the basil, garlic, pine nuts, Parmesan cheese, lemon zest, lemon juice, olive oil, salt, and pepper until the mixture is smooth and thick. Taste and season with more salt and pepper if needed. Transfer to a bowl and cover with plastic wrap. Keep in the refrigerator until ready to use.

TO MAKE THE SHRIMP KABOBS

2. Preheat an outdoor grill on medium-high or use a grill pan on your stove.

3. On a baking sheet, toss the tomatoes, summer squash, zucchini, onion, and shrimp with the garlic, red pepper flakes, olive oil, salt, and pepper. Using 8 (10-inch) metal skewers, thread 3 shrimp per skewer, alternating them with a tomato, summer squash, zucchini, and piece of red onion. Repeat, threading the other skewers with the remaining shrimp and vegetables.

4. Brush the vegetable oil on the grill grates or grill pan with a heatproof silicone brush and lay the kabobs across. Cook until the shrimp are done and the vegetables have charred, about 3 to 4 minutes per side. Transfer to a warmed plate. Tent with foil for 5 minutes. Serve the kabobs with the pesto drizzled over the top.

Freshly ground black pepper

**2 tablespoons vegetable oil,
for brushing the grill**

PRO TIP: Use metal skewers rather than wood when cooking on a grill—you won't need to soak them ahead of time, and the metal will conduct the heat through the food to help it cook faster.

PER SERVING: Calories: 697; Total fat: 60g; Protein: 36g; Carbohydrates: 13g; Fiber: 3g; Sugar: 4g; Sodium: 420mg

DRUNKEN CRAB WITH GARLIC FRIED RICE

NUT-FREE / 30 MINUTE
SERVES 4 / PREP TIME: 15 MINUTES / COOK TIME: 15 MINUTES

Make this recipe when crab is in season—you won't regret it! It's on the lighter side, braised in wine, so please do not skimp on the butter or garlic when frying the rice. You'll need it for balance, plus it's delicious.

FOR THE FRIED RICE

2 tablespoons vegetable oil

1 egg, beaten

6 garlic cloves, finely minced

2 teaspoons minced
   fresh ginger

2 cups cooked white rice

1 tablespoon soy sauce

4 tablespoons unsalted butter,
   at room temperature

4 scallions, thinly sliced

Kosher salt

Freshly ground black pepper

FOR THE CRAB

1 whole fresh Dungeness crab
   (about 2 pounds)

½ cup low-sodium
   chicken broth

1 (3-inch) piece fresh ginger,
   sliced into ¼-inch-thick coins

3 garlic cloves,
   roughly chopped

1 teaspoon fish sauce

1 tablespoon oyster sauce

1 teaspoon brown sugar

TO MAKE THE FRIED RICE

1. Heat the oil in a wok or nonstick pan over medium-high heat. When the oil is just beginning to smoke, add the egg and quickly scramble it. Add the garlic and ginger, and sauté until the garlic is fragrant, about 1 minute. Add the rice, breaking up any lumps with a spatula and tossing with the egg and garlic. Fry for 2 minutes, pressing the rice against the pan.

2. Push the rice to the sides, leaving space in the center, and add the soy sauce and butter, stirring together while the butter melts. Add the scallions and toss everything together. Taste and season lightly with salt and pepper. Set aside and keep warm.

TO MAKE THE CRAB

3. Scrub the crab all over with a brush under cold running water. Pull off the top shell and set aside. Scrub the body and pull off the gills and discard them. Cut the crab in half, and cut each half again to make quarters.

4. In a Dutch oven over high heat, bring the chicken broth, ginger, garlic, fish sauce, oyster sauce, brown sugar, and salt and pepper to a boil and add the crab (shell, too). Simmer covered for 4 to 5 minutes, or until the shell turns bright red. Lower the heat to medium-high and add the rice wine and lager. Simmer for 5 more minutes with the cover off to reduce the liquid.

Kosher salt

Freshly ground black pepper

½ cup dry Shaoxing rice wine

½ cup pale lager (such
as an IPA)

Chopped cilantro, for garnish
(optional)

5. Transfer the crab to a wide, shallow serving bowl and arrange the shell and legs back to what it looked like when it was "whole." Spoon the sauce over. Serve hot with the garlic fried rice and garnish with chopped cilantro (if using).

PREPARATION TIP: Keep the rice in the skillet on low heat, especially if you are using a nonstick pan, as you cook the crab. The rice will develop a crispy, crunchy texture.

INGREDIENT TIP: Serving a whole crab is dramatic and show-stopping, but you can simmer any fresh crab that is available. King crab legs, stone crab claws, or even smaller blue crabs would be terrific.

PER SERVING: Calories: 387; Total fat: 20g; Protein: 13g; Carbohydrates: 29g; Fiber: 1g; Sugar: 1g; Sodium: 704mg

GRILLED MACKEREL WITH DUKKAH AND LEMON

GLUTEN-FREE / DAIRY-FREE

SERVES 4 / PREP TIME: 15 MINUTES / COOK TIME: 20 MINUTES

Dukkah is an Egyptian condiment that doesn't really have a recipe—it's just a combination of toasted nuts and spices crushed or pounded into a coarse mixture. It's enjoyed by dipping bread into olive oil, then dipping into the dukkah. I love it as a garnish for fish or roasted vegetables.

FOR THE DUKKAH

2 tablespoons roughly chopped hazelnuts

2 tablespoons roughly chopped cashews

¼ cup pistachios, shelled

2 tablespoons slivered almonds

2 teaspoons coriander seeds

2 teaspoons cumin seeds

2 teaspoons sesame seeds

1 teaspoon fennel seeds

¼ teaspoon red pepper flakes

½ teaspoon kosher salt

FOR THE MACKEREL

4 mackerel fillets, skin on, deboned and butterflied

2 tablespoons extra-virgin olive oil

Kosher salt

Freshly ground black pepper

Juice of ½ lemon

TO MAKE THE DUKKAH

1. In a small skillet over medium heat, toast the hazelnuts, cashews, pistachios, and almonds for 5 minutes, or until they begin to brown and become fragrant. Transfer to a food processor.

2. Return the pan to the heat and toast the coriander, cumin, sesame, and fennel seeds until the spices are fragrant and begin to jump, about 3 minutes. Transfer to the food processor and add the red pepper flakes and salt. Pulse until the nuts and seeds are coarsely chopped. Transfer to a bowl and set aside.

TO MAKE THE MACKEREL

3. Heat a grill pan over high heat until it starts to smoke. Brush the mackerel with oil and season with salt and pepper. Sear for 3 to 4 minutes on each side, or until the skin is crispy and the flesh has dark grill marks.

4. Remove the fish from the grill and transfer to warmed plates. Drizzle the lemon juice over each fillet and top with spoonfuls of the dukkah. Serve hot.

INGREDIENT TIP: Save yourself some time and buy the mackerel fillets already butterflied from the seafood counter. Mackerel is a delectably oily fish that can handle being cooked at high, aggressive heat, so don't worry about overcooking it. The point is to infuse smoky, grilled flavor into the fish and let the nutty, spicy dukkah and lemon juice do the rest of the work for you.

PER SERVING: Calories: 416; Total fat: 33g; Protein: 25g; Carbohydrates: 8g; Fiber: 3g; Sugar: 1g; Sodium: 433mg

JAMAICAN JERK TILAPIA WITH COCONUT RICE

GLUTEN-FREE / DAIRY-FREE / NUT-FREE

SERVES 4 / PREP TIME: 15 MINUTES, PLUS 1 HOUR TO MARINATE / COOK TIME: 30 MINUTES

Caribbean jerk seasoning, which features intense heat from chiles and deeper warmth from spices, is a great marinade for fish, pork, and chicken. I'll admit this recipe is quite involved, but it's worth it. The coconut rice is more than a tasty bonus—it also works to temper the heat from the jerk marinade.

FOR THE MARINADE

½ Scotch bonnet pepper, seeded and roughly chopped

2 scallions, roughly chopped

2 garlic cloves, smashed

¼-inch piece of peeled fresh ginger

¼ cup freshly squeezed lime juice

2 packed tablespoons brown sugar

1 tablespoon allspice berries, crushed

½ teaspoon ground cinnamon

½ teaspoon whole black peppercorns

½ teaspoon kosher salt

2 tablespoons vegetable oil

2 tilapia fillets, 7 to 8 ounces each, cut into 4 equal pieces

TO MAKE THE MARINADE

1. In a blender or food processor, add the Scotch bonnet pepper, scallions, garlic, ginger, lime juice, brown sugar, allspice, cinnamon, peppercorns, and salt. Pulse until all the ingredients are finely chopped but not blended. Stir in the vegetable oil.

2. Marinate the tilapia for up to 1 hour in the refrigerator.

TO MAKE THE RICE

3. In a large saucepan stir the rice, salt, coconut milk, and water, and bring to a boil on high heat. Once at a boil, lower the heat to the lowest setting and cover. Simmer on low for 15 to 20 minutes, or until rice is tender. Set aside.

TO MAKE THE TILAPIA

4. Preheat the oven to 400°F.

5. Rub the vegetable oil in the bottom of an 8-by-8-inch baking dish. Lift the fillets out of the marinade, allowing the excess sauce to drip off, and place in the baking dish. Bake for 8 to 10 minutes, or until flaky. Remove from the oven and tent with foil.

FOR THE RICE

1 cup jasmine rice, rinsed thoroughly

½ teaspoon kosher salt

1 (14-ounce) can light coconut milk

½ cup water

FOR THE TILAPIA

1 tablespoon vegetable oil

1 lime cut into 4 wedges

6. To serve, fluff the rice with a fork and transfer to a warmed platter. Place the fish on top and serve with the lime wedges to squeeze over each fillet.

PREPARATION TIP: Make a large batch of the marinade and keep it in an airtight jar in your refrigerator; use it on chicken, shrimp, pork, or vegetables.

PER SERVING: Calories: 445; Total fat: 19g; Protein: 25g; Carbohydrates: 50g; Fiber: 1g; Sugar: 8g; Sodium: 680mg

ROASTED SARDINES WITH RED PEPPERS AND ONIONS

GLUTEN-FREE / DAIRY-FREE / NUT-FREE / 30 MINUTE / ONE POT
SERVES 2 TO 4 / PREP TIME: 10 MINUTES / COOK TIME: 20 MINUTES

I enjoyed a similar dish while in Spain, and since then I've tried re-creating it but ended up with this version, which I like even more! Red bell peppers and sardines make a surprisingly delicious combination. Don't believe me? Well, then, I guess you'll have to try this to see for yourself!

1 medium yellow onion, cut into long thin strips

1 large red bell pepper, cored and cut into ¼-inch-wide strips

3 garlic cloves, minced

4 tablespoons extra-virgin olive oil, divided

Kosher salt

Freshly ground black pepper

4 fresh sardines, butterflied and deboned

1 teaspoon ground cumin

1 teaspoon ground coriander

½ teaspoon ground turmeric

Juice of ½ lemon

Chopped parsley, for garnish (optional)

1. Preheat the oven to 425°F.

2. In a medium bowl, toss together the onion, pepper, garlic, and 1 tablespoon of olive oil, and season with salt and pepper. Transfer to a 9-by-13-inch baking dish.

3. Season the sardines on all sides with salt and pepper. Drizzle with 1 tablespoon of olive oil and arrange the sardines over the vegetables, opened flat in the center.

4. In a small bowl, stir together the cumin, coriander, turmeric, lemon juice, and remaining 2 tablespoons of olive oil. Season with salt and pepper. Pour the sauce over the sardines and vegetables.

5. Bake for 15 minutes, or until the vegetables are tender. Switch the oven to broil. Flip the sardines skin-side up, then broil for 5 minutes, or until the skins are crispy. Serve immediately and garnish with a bit of chopped parsley (if using).

INGREDIENT TIP: Buy the sardines already butterflied from the seafood counter and save yourself some time.

SUBSTITUTION TIP: You can swap the sardines for any flaky fish you like: snapper, tilapia, catfish, trout, or even halibut.

PER SERVING: Calories: 367; Total fat: 31g; Protein: 13g; Carbohydrates: 13g; Fiber: 3g; Sugar: 5g; Sodium: 6mg

MISO-LACQUERED BLACK COD

GLUTEN-FREE / NUT-FREE / ONE POT
SERVES 4 / PREP TIME: 40 MINUTES / COOK TIME: 15 MINUTES

Buttery black cod coated in a sweet and savory glaze served slightly bruléed is a show-stopping dish for company. It looks really advanced, but don't worry—it couldn't be easier.

4 (5 to 6 ounce) black cod fillets

Kosher salt

Freshly ground black pepper

¼ cup miso paste

¼ cup dark brown sugar

2 teaspoons toasted sesame oil

2 tablespoons mirin

2 teaspoons mayonnaise

1. Line a baking sheet with aluminum foil and set aside.

2. Blot the fish with a paper towel and season lightly with salt and pepper.

3. In a small bowl, combine the miso, brown sugar, sesame oil, and mirin. Stir together until the brown sugar is dissolved. Stir in the mayonnaise until fully combined.

4. Brush 1 or 2 tablespoons of the miso mixture over each piece of fish, saving half the marinade for later. Marinate for at least 30 minutes, or up to 1 hour.

5. Preheat the oven to 375°F.

6. Roast the fish for 7 to 8 minutes, or until opaque and slightly flaky. Switch the oven to broil. Brush the remainder of the glaze over the pieces and broil for 2 minutes, or until the tops are caramelized and slightly charred. Remove from the oven and tent with foil for 5 minutes.

7. Plate the fish on warmed dinner plates and serve hot.

SERVING TIP: Garnish with 2 tablespoons of roasted sesame seeds, 1 tablespoon of roughly chopped cilantro, and 2 thinly sliced scallions.

INGREDIENT TIP: Black cod has a few other names depending on where you live: sablefish, butterfish, and blue cod, so don't worry if you can't find it right away.

PER SERVING: Calories: 260; Total fat: 5g; Protein: 32g; Carbohydrates: 22g; Fiber: 0g; Sugar: 11g; Sodium: 731mg

LOBSTER MAC AND CHEESE

NUT-FREE
SERVES 6 TO 8 / PREP TIME: 30 MINUTES, PLUS 40 MINUTES TO CHILL /
COOK TIME: 1 HOUR 5 MINUTES

If you are craving comfort food but also are feeling spendy, take this recipe for a spin! It takes extra work, but the results are worth it. This recipe requires live lobsters to be cooked, so if you'd rather not do that, that's okay. Simply buy cooked lobster—it'll still be great, and you'll save some time.

2 (2-pound) live lobsters
   or 1½ pounds cooked
   lobster meat

½ cup kosher salt, divided,
   plus additional for seasoning

1 quart whole milk

12 tablespoons (1½ sticks)
   unsalted butter, divided

1 pound dried cavatappi pasta

1½ cups panko bread crumbs

½ cup all-purpose flour

Pinch cayenne pepper

1 tablespoon Dijon mustard

4 cups grated Gruyère cheese

2 cups grated sharp
   Cheddar cheese

2 tablespoons roughly
   chopped flat leaf parsley

1. Fill a large bowl with ice water and set aside.

2. Use the tip of a very sharp and heavy chef knife to dispatch the lobsters. Drive the tip straight into the crack on the head, behind the eyes.

3. Bring a large stock pot of water to a rolling boil and add ¼ cup of salt. Lower the lobsters into the water and cook until they turn bright red, about 5 to 7 minutes.

4. Use kitchen tongs to lift the lobsters from the pot and immediately plunge them into the ice water. Chill for 10 minutes, then drain.

5. When the lobsters are cold, remove the tails and claws and discard the bodies (or use for another recipe). Crack the shells from the tails and claws and remove the meat, holding onto the shells. Trim out the vein that runs down the tail and cut the meat into ½-inch chunks. Place the meat in a strainer set over a bowl to catch the excess liquid, and chill in the refrigerator for at least 30 minutes. Save the shells to simmer in the milk.

6. Preheat the oven to 375°F.

7. In a large saucepan over medium heat, simmer the milk and lobster shells together for 10 to 12 minutes.

8. Butter the bottom and sides of a deep 3-quart casserole dish with 2 tablespoons of butter. Set aside.

9. Fill the stockpot with fresh water and bring to a boil over high heat. Add ¼ cup of salt and cook the pasta according to package directions. Drain and set aside.

10. Return the stockpot to the stove and melt the remaining 10 tablespoons of butter over medium heat. Remove 2 tablespoons of butter and stir them into a small bowl along with the bread crumbs, then set aside. Whisk the flour and cayenne pepper into the butter in the stockpot. Continue stirring until the flour begins to smell nutty, about 2 to 3 minutes. Stir in the Dijon mustard and season with a generous pinch of salt.

11. Strain the milk directly into the stockpot and discard the lobster shells. Increase the heat to medium-high and continue whisking as it comes to a boil; it will become smooth and thick in about 5 to 7 minutes. Stir in the Gruyère cheese, Cheddar cheese, and cooked pasta. Taste and add more salt if needed. Fold in the chopped lobster and transfer to the baking dish.

12. Stir the parsley with a pinch of salt into the bread crumbs and sprinkle all over the top of the mac and cheese. Bake for 20 to 25 minutes, or until the mac and cheese is bubbly and the bread crumbs have browned. Remove from the oven and let it sit for 5 to 10 minutes before serving.

PREPARATION TIP: Break up the recipe into smaller do-ahead chunks. Cook and shell the lobster a couple of days in advance. Simmer the milk and cook the pasta ahead, too. Assemble the day you want to serve it, and serve hot, right from the oven.

PER SERVING: Calories: 1,210; Total fat: 65g; Protein: 68g; Carbohydrates: 94g; Fiber: 4g; Sugar: 11g; Sodium: 10,364mg

MEASUREMENTS AND CONVERSIONS

VOLUME EQUIVALENTS (LIQUID)

US STANDARD	US STANDARD (OUNCES)	METRIC (APPROXIMATE)
2 tablespoons	1 fl. oz.	30 mL
¼ cup	2 fl. oz.	60 mL
½ cup	4 fl. oz.	120 mL
1 cup	8 fl. oz.	240 mL
1½ cups	12 fl. oz.	355 mL
2 cups or 1 pint	16 fl. oz.	475 mL
4 cups or 1 quart	32 fl. oz.	1 L
1 gallon	128 fl. oz.	4 L

OVEN TEMPERATURES

FAHRENHEIT	CELSIUS (APPROXIMATE)
250°F	120°C
300°F	150°C
325°F	165°C
350°F	180°C
375°F	190°C
400°F	200°C
425°F	220°C
450°F	230°C

VOLUME EQUIVALENTS (DRY)

US STANDARD	METRIC (APPROXIMATE)
⅛ teaspoon	0.5 mL
¼ teaspoon	1 mL
½ teaspoon	2 mL
¾ teaspoon	4 mL
1 teaspoon	5 mL
1 tablespoon	15 mL
¼ cup	59 mL
⅓ cup	79 mL
½ cup	118 mL
⅔ cup	156 mL
¾ cup	177 mL
1 cup	235 mL
2 cups or 1 pint	475 mL
3 cups	700 mL
4 cups or 1 quart	1 L

WEIGHT EQUIVALENTS

US STANDARD	METRIC (APPROXIMATE)
½ ounce	15 g
1 ounce	30 g
2 ounces	60 g
4 ounces	115 g
8 ounces	225 g
12 ounces	340 g
16 ounces or 1 pound	455 g

RESOURCES

Environmental Defense Fund Seafood Selector: EDF is a nonprofit environmental advocacy group based in the US. The group focuses on issues such as global warming, ecosystem restoration, the oceans, and human health. Their Seafood Selector is a tool to help you become a better-informed consumer of sustainable seafood. **seafood.edf.org**

The Food Lab: "How to Kill, Cook, and Shell a Lobster" is a great article on how to cook a live lobster, which is necessary for the freshest possible taste in any recipe that calls for lobster. **seriouseats.com/2013/05/the-food-lab-how-to-cook-shuck-lobster.html**

Marine Stewardship Council: This is a global nonprofit organization, based in London, that sets standards for sustainable fishing. Their website provides a host of information for consumers to make sustainable choices when shopping for seafood. **msc.org**

Monterey Bay Aquarium Seafood Watch: Seafood Watch, a program run by the Monterey Bay Aquarium, is one of the best-known sites for consumers to look up information about eco-friendly seafood so they can make informed decisions on purchasing seafood or ordering in restaurants. **seafoodwatch.org**

Ocean Conservancy: This is a nonprofit environmental advocacy group, based in Washington, DC, which advocates policies that help protect marine wildlife. **oceanconservancy.org**

GLOSSARY

BLACK COD: Also known as sablefish, blue cod, or butterfish, this is a deep sea fish of the Pacific Ocean. It is a firm, flaky whitefish perfect for grilling, searing, roasting, and frying. Its levels of omega-3s are as high as those of wild salmon.

CALAMARI: Also known as squid, calamari is its culinary name. A cephalopod from the mollusk family, calamari are prepared fried or added to stews and soups. Even their ink, which they use for defense, is used in culinary applications, added to rice and pasta.

CATFISH: Catfish is "the King of Soul Food," with its roots going all the way back to colonial times. When the cotton industry collapsed, farmers in southern states decided to flood their cotton fields and farm catfish instead. An extremely versatile whitefish, its mild flavor can stand up to nearly every flavor profile, from simple fried recipes to spicy stews and everything in between.

CLAMS: Clams can be broken down into two major categories: hard shell and soft shell. Hard shell clams come in a variety of sizes; from the smallest to the largest they are: Manila, littleneck, cherrystone, chowder, and quahog. The smaller they are, the more tender and sweet they are; the larger ones are tougher and should be chopped up before adding to a recipe.

COD: Cod is a dense, flaky whitefish with a mild flavor and high levels of vitamins A, D, and E, and of omega-3s. Cod is a versatile fish from the northern Atlantic Ocean and very common in European cuisines dating back to the time of the Vikings.

CRAB: Crab is enjoyed as a delicacy all over the world. Some species are eaten whole, while just the legs and claws of other species are eaten. Crab is popular in Asian cuisines as well as on the eastern and southern coasts of the United States.

HADDOCK: Haddock is related to cod and is sold as scrod in Massachusetts. Its meat is white and firm with nice large flakes perfect for frying, roasting, broiling, and sautéing.

HALIBUT: Halibut is a whitefish with a mild flavor and a firm, dense texture. It cooks well in deep frying, grilling, steaming, sautéing, and broiling. Eaten fresh, the meat has a clean taste and requires little seasoning.

LOBSTER: Lobsters are the largest crustaceans we eat. They turn red or coral colored when cooked, and their meat is sweet and succulent. Their name is from the Old English *loppe*, which means "spider." Lobster is enjoyed mostly in North America and Asia, and is best sautéed or steamed. Females are called hens, and males are called cocks—just like chickens!

MACKEREL: A relative of tuna, mackerel is a beautiful fish in its own right. Its skin is a luminous iridescent striped or spotty pattern (depending on the type), and its meat is rich and oily. When cooked, mackerel has a rich and fishy flavor with white flaky meat.

MAHI-MAHI: Mahi-mahi, also known as dolphinfish, is a firm, lean white tropical fish found near Hawaii and the Gulf of Mexico. It is a less expensive alternative to halibut and can be grilled, broiled, or even fried.

MUSSELS: Mussels are an affordable way to enjoy wonderfully delicious and easy seafood. The most widely available mussels at the market are the blue mussels farm raised (or cultivated) on Prince Edward Island (PEI), Canada. The PEI designation indicates reliable high quality, good flavor, and sustainably abundant supply. In fact, due to their water-filtering capabilities, mussels are considered eco-friendly.

OYSTERS: Oysters, which are bivalve mollusks related to clams and mussels, are some of the most versatile of all seafood and can be enjoyed raw from the shell, grilled, steamed, or fried, and they can be incorporated into dozens of dishes and cuisines. Oyster farms have a low impact on the natural environment and are managed to ensure high sustainability.

SALMON: Salmon, available from both the Atlantic and Pacific Oceans, are anadromous, meaning they are born in freshwater, then migrate to salt water, then return to freshwater to spawn. It can be broiled, roasted, grilled, poached, steamed, smoked, or fried and is likely the most popular of all the fish we consume. It's appealing to many due to its mild flavor, firm texture, high nutritional value, and gorgeous color—and it's never out of season.

SARDINES: Sardines are abundant in the Atlantic and Pacific Oceans and the Mediterranean Sea. They feed on plankton only, which means their mercury levels are relatively low. Fresh sardines are fabulous grilled, broiled, roasted, and fried. Canned sardines, especially ones packed in oil, are great in salads.

SCALLOPS: Scallops, like oysters, are bivalve mollusks related to clams and mussels but with a more delicate texture and flavor. They are best broiled, seared, roasted, and fried. There are two kinds: bay scallops and sea scallops; sea scallops are larger and meatier.

SEA BASS: Sea bass is a meaty but lean whitefish that is great for grilling and broiling. Sea bass, like black sea bass or Chilean sea bass, is a saltwater fish, whereas striped bass is a freshwater fish.

SHRIMP: Shrimp are the smallest of the crustaceans and are found in oceans all over the world. They're not only very nutritious, but they are the most popular shellfish in the United States. Shrimp are available year round and are a popular ingredient in appetizers, sandwiches, salads, chowders, and entrées.

SOLE: Generally speaking, sole is a name for any flatfish, such as members of the flounder family. Dover sole is the most widely available and is great served broiled, pan-seared, or poached.

TILAPIA: Tilapia is an inexpensive freshwater whitefish that is mild in flavor with a firm and flaky texture. It's a great fish to start with if you're new to cooking fish at home. Tilapia goes well with so many different flavor profiles and is widely available in supermarkets across the country in both fresh and frozen options—it really should be called the "chicken of the sea." It's a freshwater fish so it doesn't taste or smell very "fishy."

TROUT: Trout, like catfish, is a large commercial industry in North America, dating back to the 1880s when the first trout hatchery was founded. The meat of the rainbow trout is delicate, tender, and flaky with a mild and subtle nutty flavor. When shopping, choose sustainably farmed trout from the northern United States.

TUNA: Tuna is a very popular fish to consume, and because of that it's in danger of being overfished, according to the World Wildlife Foundation. Nevertheless, there are many ways to enjoy tuna, from classic comfort food recipes to more adventurous dishes. Skipjack tuna, the smallest of the species, is in larger supply and has the lowest amounts of mercury.

REFERENCES

American Heart Association. "Fish and Omega-3 Fatty Acids." Accessed February 1, 2020. https://www.heart.org/en/healthy-living/healthy-eating/eat-smart/fats/fish-and-omega-3-fatty-acids.

American Society for Nutrition. "Is Fish Smelly?" Accessed February 1, 2020. https://nutrition.org/is-fish-smelly.

Bradford, Alina. "Mercury Poisoning: Causes, Effects, and Fish." February 25, 2016. *Live Science*. https://www.livescience.com/53837-mercury-poisoning.html.

Fred Hutchinson Cancer Research Center. "Eskimo Study Suggests High Consumption of Omega-3s in Fish-Rich Diet Reduces Obesity-Related Disease Risk." *ScienceDaily*. March 25, 2011. https://www.sciencedaily.com/releases/2011/03/110324153712.htm.

Healthline. "11 Evidence-Based Health Benefits of Eating Fish." Accessed February 1, 2020. https://www.healthline.com/nutrition/11-health-benefits-of-fish#section1.

Hobson, Katherine, and Allison Underhill. "13 Best Fish: High in Omega-3s—and Environment Friendly." *US News & World Report*. Accessed February 1, 2020. https://health.usnews.com/wellness/slideshows/13-best-fish-high-in-omega-3sand-environment-friendly.

J. J. McDonnell. "Benefits Far Outweigh the Risks of Eating Fish." Accessed February 1, 2020. http://www.jjmcdonnell.com/product-information/seafood-good-for-you.

National Resources Defense Council. "Mercury Guide." Accessed February 1, 2020. https://www.nrdc.org/stories/mercury-guide.

Ocean Wise. "Sustainable Seafood." Accessed February 1, 2020. https://seafood.ocean.org/sustainable-seafood.

Office of Disease Prevention. "2015–2020 Dietary Guidelines." Accessed February 1, 2020. https://health.gov/dietaryguidelines/2015.

UCLA Medical Center. "Boost Your Brain: Things to Do, Eat and Drink Which Could Stave Off Alzheimer's." Accessed February 1, 2020. https://teplowlab.neurology.ucla.edu/index.php/news/17-boost-your-brain-things-to-do-eat-and-drink-which-could-stave-off-alzheimer-s.

World Wildlife Foundation. "Species: Tuna." Accessed February 1, 2020. https://www.worldwildlife.org/species/tuna.

INDEX

A

Anchovies
  Pan Bagnat (Provençal Tuna
    Sandwiches), 81
  Spaghetti with Clams, 96–97
Appetizers
  Ceviche, 45
  Chinese Shrimp
    Toast, 52–53
  Clams Casino, 48–49
  Classic Crab Cakes, 34
  Crab Potstickers, 38–39
  Crab Rangoons, 47
  Layered California Sushi
    Dip, 40–41
  Salmon Mousse, 43
  Smoked Salmon Deviled
    Eggs, 51
  Summer Rolls, 54
Apple and Smoked Trout
  Salad, 50
Aquaculture, 3, 5
Asparagus
  Shrimp Louie, 35
Avocados
  Layered California Sushi
    Dip, 40–41
  Shrimp and Papaya
    Salad, 42
  Shrimp Louie, 35
  Smoked Salmon with Baked
    Eggs in Avocados, 28

B

Bacon
  Broiled Shrimp Scampi with
    Crumbled Bacon, 91
  Cajun Catfish and Spinach
    Stew, 99

Clams Casino, 48–49
Hangtown Fry, 22–23
New England Clam
  Chowder, 60–61
Smoked Oyster Soup, 67
Smoked Trout and Bacon
  Cornmeal Waffles, 27
Bang Bang Shrimp in Lettuce
  Cups, 90
Beans
  Cajun Catfish and Spinach
    Stew, 99
Beer
  Classic British Fish and
    Chips, 86–87
  Drunken Crab with Garlic
    Fried Rice, 132–133
Blackened Catfish, 108–109
Bouillabaisse, 75–76
Broiled Halibut with
  Lemon-Herb
  Persillade, 123
Broiled Shrimp Scampi with
  Crumbled Bacon, 91
Broiling, 13

C

Cabbage
  Bang Bang Shrimp in
    Lettuce Cups, 90
  Crab Potstickers, 38–39
Cajun Catfish and Spinach
  Stew, 99
Carrots
  Bang Bang Shrimp in
    Lettuce Cups, 90
  Crab Bisque, 62–63
  Fish Tacos with Pickled
    Vegetables, 102–103

Pistachio-Crusted Tuna and
  Lentil Salad, 128–129
Shrimp Banh Mi
  Sandwiches, 77–78
Summer Rolls, 54
Thai-Spiced Salmon Fillet en
  Papillote, 114–115
Catfish
  Blackened Catfish, 108–109
  Cajun Catfish and Spinach
    Stew, 99
Celery
  Cajun Catfish and Spinach
    Stew, 99
  Classic Creole Shrimp
    Gumbo, 64–65
  Lobster Roll, 69–70
  New England Clam
    Chowder, 60–61
  Open-Faced Tuna Melts, 66
  Salmon Hash with Fried
    Eggs, 26
  Scallop and Clam Pan
    Roast, 111
  Tuna Noodle
    Casserole, 100–101
Ceviche, 45
Cheese. See also
    Cream cheese
  Chilaquiles with Sautéed
    Shrimp, 30–31
  Clams Casino, 48–49
  Crab Strata with Pimentos
    and Cheese, 24–25
  Grilled Shrimp Kabobs with
    Pesto Sauce, 130–131
  Lobster Mac and
    Cheese, 140–141
  Open-Faced Tuna Melts, 66

Chilaquiles with Sautéed Shrimp, 30–31

Chilean Sea Bass with Roasted Lemons and Fresh Herbs, 92

Chiles
Summer Rolls, 54
Thai-Spiced Salmon Fillet en Papillote, 114–115

Chinese Shrimp Toast, 52–53

Cioppino, 73–74

Clams
Cioppino, 73–74
Clams Casino, 48–49
New England Clam Chowder, 60–61
Scallop and Clam Pan Roast, 111
Seafood Paella, 94–95
Spaghetti with Clams, 96–97

Classic British Fish and Chips, 86–87

Classic Crab Cakes, 34

Classic Creole Shrimp Gumbo, 64–65

Coconut milk
Jamaican Jerk Tilapia with Coconut Rice, 136–137
Spicy Thai Coconut Shrimp Soup, 68

Cod
Classic British Fish and Chips, 86–87
Cod in Spiced Tomato Curry, 126
Fish Tacos with Pickled Vegetables, 102–103
Miso-Lacquered Black Cod, 139

Cooking methods, 12–13

Corn
Lowcountry Boil, 98

Crab
Cioppino, 73–74
Classic Crab Cakes, 34
Crab Bisque, 62–63
Crab Potstickers, 38–39
Crab Rangoons, 47
Crab Strata with Pimentos and Cheese, 24–25
Drunken Crab with Garlic Fried Rice, 132–133
Layered California Sushi Dip, 40–41

Cream cheese
Crab Rangoons, 47

Cucumbers
Seared Ahi Tuna Niçoise Salad, 36–37
Shrimp Banh Mi Sandwiches, 77–78

D

Dairy-free
Cajun Catfish and Spinach Stew, 99
Ceviche, 45
Chilean Sea Bass with Roasted Lemons and Fresh Herbs, 92
Cioppino, 73–74
Classic British Fish and Chips, 86–87
Classic Creole Shrimp Gumbo, 64–65
Crab Potstickers, 38–39
Fried Calamari with Rustic Tomato Sauce, 104–105
Fried Sardines with Gremolata, 121–122
Grilled Mackerel with Dukkah and Lemon, 134–135
Jamaican Jerk Tilapia with Coconut Rice, 136–137
Pistachio-Crusted Tuna and Lentil Salad, 128–129

Red Snapper Veracruz, 127

Roasted Sardines with Red Peppers and Onions, 138

Salmon Teriyaki, 106

Sardine and Pimento Bocadillos, 79

Seafood Paella, 94–95

Shrimp and Orzo Salad, 46

Shrimp and Papaya Salad, 42

Spicy Fideos with Mussels, 88–89

Spicy Thai Coconut Shrimp Soup, 68

Summer Rolls, 54

Thai-Spiced Salmon Fillet en Papillote, 114–115

Deep frying, 13

Drunken Crab with Garlic Fried Rice, 132–133

E

Eggs
Chilaquiles with Sautéed Shrimp, 30–31
Crab Strata with Pimentos and Cheese, 24–25
Drunken Crab with Garlic Fried Rice, 132–133
Hangtown Fry, 22–23
Pan Bagnat (Provençal Tuna Sandwiches), 81
Salmon Hash with Fried Eggs, 26
Seared Ahi Tuna Niçoise Salad, 36–37
Shrimp Louie, 35
Shrimp Omelets, 18–19
Smoked Mackerel Kedgeree, 20–21
Smoked Salmon Benedict, 16–17
Smoked Salmon Deviled Eggs, 51

Eggs (*continued*)
    Smoked Salmon with
        Baked Eggs in
        Avocados, 28
    Tuna and Tomato
        Frittata, 29
Equipment, 7–8

F

Fennel
    Cioppino, 73–74
    Steamed Mussels with
        White Wine and
        Fennel, 110
Finfish, 8–9
Fish. *See also specific*
    benefits of consuming, 2
    canned, 10
    farmed vs. wild, 3, 5
    finfish, 8–9
    freshwater vs. saltwater, 3
    frozen, 10–11
    odor elimination, 4
    prepping, 11–12
    shellfish, 9
    shopping for, 9–11
    storing, 11–12
Fish Tacos with Pickled
        Vegetables, 102–103
5 ingredient
    Shrimp Omelets, 18–19
Freezer staples, 7
Fried Calamari with
        Rustic Tomato
        Sauce, 104–105
Fried Sardines with
        Gremolata, 121–122

G

Gluten-free
    Bang Bang Shrimp in
        Lettuce Cups, 90
    Ceviche, 45

Chilaquiles with Sautéed
        Shrimp, 30–31
Chilean Sea Bass with
        Roasted Lemons and
        Fresh Herbs, 92
Cioppino, 73–74
Cod in Spiced Tomato
        Curry, 126
Fish Tacos with Pickled
        Vegetables, 102–103
Grilled Mackerel with
        Dukkah and
        Lemon, 134–135
Grilled Shrimp Kabobs
        with Pesto
        Sauce, 130–131
Grilled Tuna Steaks with
        Wasabi Butter, 125
Jamaican Jerk Tilapia
        with Coconut
        Rice, 136–137
Layered California Sushi
        Dip, 40–41
Lowcountry Boil, 98
Miso-Lacquered Black
        Cod, 139
Red Snapper Veracruz, 127
Roasted Salmon with
        Lemon-Garlic Butter, 119
Roasted Sardines with Red
        Peppers and Onions, 138
Salmon Hash with Fried
        Eggs, 26
Salmon Mousse, 43
Seafood Paella, 94–95
Seared Ahi Tuna Niçoise
        Salad, 36–37
Seared Scallops with
        Pineapple Beurre
        Blanc, 112–113
Shrimp and Papaya
        Salad, 42
Shrimp Louie, 35
Shrimp Omelets, 18–19

Smoked Mackerel
        Kedgeree, 20–21
Smoked Oyster Soup, 67
Smoked Salmon Deviled
        Eggs, 51
Smoked Trout and Apple
        Salad, 50
Spicy Thai Coconut Shrimp
        Soup, 68
Summer Rolls, 54
Thai-Spiced Salmon Fillet en
        Papillote, 114–115
Green beans
    Seared Ahi Tuna Niçoise
        Salad, 36–37
Greens. *See also specific*
    Seared Ahi Tuna Niçoise
        Salad, 36–37
    Smoked Trout and Apple
        Salad, 50
Grilled Mackerel with
        Dukkah and
        Lemon, 134–135
Grilled Shrimp Kabobs
        with Pesto
        Sauce, 130–131
Grilled Tuna Steaks with
        Wasabi Butter, 125
Grilling, 13

H

Haddock
    Classic British Fish and
        Chips, 86–87
Halibut
    Broiled Halibut with
        Lemon-Herb
        Persillade, 123
    Seafood Paella, 94–95
Ham
    Lowcountry Boil, 98
Hangtown Fry, 22–23
Health benefits, 2

I

Ingredient staples, 6–7

J

Jamaican Jerk Tilapia with
　　Coconut Rice, 136–137

L

Layered California Sushi
　　Dip, 40–41

Leeks
　　Salmon Hash with Fried
　　　　Eggs, 26
　　Smoked Oyster Soup, 67

Lemongrass
　　Shrimp Banh Mi
　　　　Sandwiches, 77–78
　　Spicy Thai Coconut Shrimp
　　　　Soup, 68
　　Thai-Spiced Salmon Fillet en
　　　　Papillote, 114–115

Lemons
　　Broiled Halibut with
　　　　Lemon-Herb
　　　　Persillade, 123
　　Chilean Sea Bass with
　　　　Roasted Lemons and
　　　　Fresh Herbs, 92
　　Grilled Mackerel with
　　　　Dukkah and
　　　　Lemon, 134–135
　　Roasted Salmon with
　　　　Lemon-Garlic Butter, 119

Lentil and Pistachio-Crusted
　　Tuna Salad, 128–129

Lettuce
　　Bang Bang Shrimp in
　　　　Lettuce Cups, 90
　　Lobster Roll, 69–70
　　Quick and Easy Oyster Po'
　　　　Boys, 58–59
　　Shrimp Louie, 35
　　Summer Rolls, 54

Lobster Mac and
　　Cheese, 140–141
Lobster Roll, 69–70
Lowcountry Boil, 98

M

Macadamia-Crusted
　　Mahi-Mahi, 118

Mackerel
　　Grilled Mackerel with
　　　　Dukkah and
　　　　Lemon, 134–135
　　Smoked Mackerel
　　　　Kedgeree, 20–21

Mahi-Mahi, Macadamia-
　　Crusted, 118

Mercury, 2–3

Miso-Lacquered Black
　　Cod, 139

Monkfish
　　Seafood Paella, 94–95

Mushrooms
　　Tuna Noodle
　　　　Casserole, 100–101

Mussels
　　Bouillabaisse, 75–76
　　Cioppino, 73–74
　　Seafood Paella, 94–95
　　Spicy Fideos with
　　　　Mussels, 88–89
　　Steamed Mussels with
　　　　White Wine and
　　　　Fennel, 110

N

New England Clam
　　Chowder, 60–61

No cook
　　Ceviche, 45
　　Pan Bagnat (Provençal Tuna
　　　　Sandwiches), 81
　　Salmon Mousse, 43

Shrimp and Papaya
　　Salad, 42
Smoked Trout and Apple
　　Salad, 50
Summer Rolls, 54

Noodles. *See also* Pasta
　　Tuna Noodle
　　　　Casserole, 100–101

Nut-free
　　Bang Bang Shrimp in
　　　　Lettuce Cups, 90
　　Blackened Catfish, 108–109
　　Bouillabaisse, 75–76
　　Broiled Halibut with
　　　　Lemon-Herb
　　　　Persillade, 123
　　Broiled Shrimp Scampi with
　　　　Crumbled Bacon, 91
　　Cajun Catfish and Spinach
　　　　Stew, 99
　　Ceviche, 45
　　Chilaquiles with Sautéed
　　　　Shrimp, 30–31
　　Chilean Sea Bass with
　　　　Roasted Lemons and
　　　　Fresh Herbs, 92
　　Chinese Shrimp
　　　　Toast, 52–53
　　Cioppino, 73–74
　　Clams Casino, 48–49
　　Classic British Fish and
　　　　Chips, 86–87
　　Classic Crab Cakes, 34
　　Classic Creole Shrimp
　　　　Gumbo, 64–65
　　Cod in Spiced Tomato
　　　　Curry, 126
　　Crab Bisque, 62–63
　　Crab Potstickers, 38–39
　　Crab Rangoons, 47
　　Crab Strata with Pimentos
　　　　and Cheese, 24–25

Nut-free (*continued*)

Drunken Crab with Garlic
Fried Rice, 132–133

Fish Tacos with Pickled
Vegetables, 102–103

Fried Calamari with Rustic
Tomato Sauce, 104–105

Fried Sardines with
Gremolata, 121–122

Grilled Tuna Steaks with
Wasabi Butter, 125

Hangtown Fry, 22–23

Jamaican Jerk Tilapia with
Coconut Rice, 136–137

Layered California Sushi
Dip, 40–41

Lobster Mac and
Cheese, 140–141

Lobster Roll, 69–70

Lowcountry Boil, 98

Miso-Lacquered Black
Cod, 139

New England Clam
Chowder, 60–61

Open-Faced Tuna Melts, 66

Oysters Rockefeller, 116–117

Pan Bagnat (Provençal Tuna
Sandwiches), 81

Quick and Easy Oyster Po'
Boys, 58–59

Red Snapper Veracruz, 127

Roasted Salmon with
Lemon-Garlic Butter, 119

Roasted Sardines with Red
Peppers and Onions, 138

Salmon Burgers, 71–72

Salmon Hash with Fried
Eggs, 26

Salmon Mousse, 43

Salmon Teriyaki, 106

Sardine and Pimento
Bocadillos, 79

Scallop and Clam Pan
Roast, 111

Seafood Paella, 94–95

Seared Ahi Tuna Niçoise
Salad, 36–37

Seared Scallops with
Pineapple Beurre
Blanc, 112–113

Shrimp and Orzo Salad, 46

Shrimp and Papaya
Salad, 42

Shrimp Banh Mi
Sandwiches, 77–78

Shrimp Louie, 35

Shrimp Omelets, 18–19

Smoked Mackerel
Kedgeree, 20–21

Smoked Oyster
Soup, 67

Smoked Salmon
Benedict, 16–17

Smoked Salmon Deviled
Eggs, 51

Smoked Salmon with
Baked Eggs in
Avocados, 28

Smoked Trout and Apple
Salad, 50

Smoked Trout and Bacon
Cornmeal Waffles, 27

Sole Meunière, 107

Spaghetti with
Clams, 96–97

Spicy Fideos with
Mussels, 88–89

Spicy Thai Coconut Shrimp
Soup, 68

Steamed Mussels with
White Wine and
Fennel, 110

Summer Rolls, 54

Thai-Spiced Salmon Fillet en
Papillote, 114–115

Trout Hand Pies, 82–83

Tuna and Tomato
Frittata, 29

Tuna Noodle
Casserole, 100–101

Nuts

Grilled Mackerel with
Dukkah and
Lemon, 134–135

Grilled Shrimp Kabobs with
Pesto Sauce, 130–131

Macadamia-Crusted
Mahi-Mahi, 118

Pistachio-Crusted Tuna and
Lentil Salad, 128–129

O

Okra

Classic Creole Shrimp
Gumbo, 64–65

Olives

Red Snapper Veracruz, 127

Seared Ahi Tuna Niçoise
Salad, 36–37

One pot

Bang Bang Shrimp in
Lettuce Cups, 90

Bouillabaisse, 75–76

Broiled Halibut with
Lemon-Herb
Persillade, 123

Broiled Shrimp Scampi with
Crumbled Bacon, 91

Cajun Catfish and Spinach
Stew, 99

Chinese Shrimp
Toast, 52–53

Cioppino, 73–74

Classic British Fish and
Chips, 86–87

Classic Crab Cakes, 34

Classic Creole Shrimp
Gumbo, 64–65

Cod in Spiced Tomato
Curry, 126

Crab Potstickers, 38–39

Crab Rangoons, 47

Fried Sardines with Gremolata, 121–122

Grilled Tuna Steaks with Wasabi Butter, 125

Hangtown Fry, 22–23

Lowcountry Boil, 98

Macadamia-Crusted Mahi-Mahi, 118

Miso-Lacquered Black Cod, 139

Open-Faced Tuna Melts, 66

Red Snapper Veracruz, 127

Roasted Salmon with Lemon-Garlic Butter, 119

Roasted Sardines with Red Peppers and Onions, 138

Salmon Burgers, 71–72

Salmon Hash with Fried Eggs, 26

Salmon Teriyaki, 106

Scallop and Clam Pan Roast, 111

Seared Ahi Tuna Niçoise Salad, 36–37

Shrimp and Orzo Salad, 46

Shrimp Banh Mi Sandwiches, 77–78

Shrimp Louie, 35

Shrimp Omelets, 18–19

Smoked Mackerel Kedgeree, 20–21

Smoked Oyster Soup, 67

Smoked Salmon Benedict, 16–17

Smoked Salmon with Baked Eggs in Avocados, 28

Smoked Trout and Bacon Cornmeal Waffles, 27

Sole Meunière, 107

Spicy Fideos with Mussels, 88–89

Spicy Thai Coconut Shrimp Soup, 68

Steamed Mussels with White Wine and Fennel, 110

Thai-Spiced Salmon Fillet en Papillote, 114–115

Tuna and Tomato Frittata, 29

Open-Faced Tuna Melts, 66

Oven roasting, 12–13

Oysters

Hangtown Fry, 22–23

Oysters Rockefeller, 116–117

Quick and Easy Oyster Po' Boys, 58–59

Smoked Oyster Soup, 67

P

Pan Bagnat (Provençal Tuna Sandwiches), 81

Pan roasting, 12

Pantry staples, 6

Papaya and Shrimp Salad, 42

Pasta

Lobster Mac and Cheese, 140–141

Shrimp and Orzo Salad, 46

Spaghetti with Clams, 96–97

Spicy Fideos with Mussels, 88–89

Peas

Seafood Paella, 94–95

Peppers

Bouillabaisse, 75–76

Cajun Catfish and Spinach Stew, 99

Chilaquiles with Sautéed Shrimp, 30–31

Clams Casino, 48–49

Classic Creole Shrimp Gumbo, 64–65

Crab Strata with Pimentos and Cheese, 24–25

Fish Tacos with Pickled Vegetables, 102–103

Jamaican Jerk Tilapia with Coconut Rice, 136–137

Pan Bagnat (Provençal Tuna Sandwiches), 81

Red Snapper Veracruz, 127

Roasted Sardines with Red Peppers and Onions, 138

Sardine and Pimento Bocadillos, 79

Shrimp and Papaya Salad, 42

Shrimp Banh Mi Sandwiches, 77–78

Spicy Thai Coconut Shrimp Soup, 68

Pistachio-Crusted Tuna and Lentil Salad, 128–129

Poaching, 13

Potatoes

Bouillabaisse, 75–76

Cajun Catfish and Spinach Stew, 99

Classic British Fish and Chips, 86–87

Lowcountry Boil, 98

New England Clam Chowder, 60–61

Salmon Hash with Fried Eggs, 26

Seared Ahi Tuna Niçoise Salad, 36–37

Smoked Oyster Soup, 67

Trout Hand Pies, 82–83

Q

Quick and Easy Oyster Po' Boys, 58–59

R

Red Snapper Veracruz, 127

Refrigerator staples, 7

Rice
  Cod in Spiced Tomato
    Curry, 126
  Drunken Crab with Garlic
    Fried Rice, 132–133
  Jamaican Jerk Tilapia with
    Coconut Rice, 136–137
  Layered California Sushi
    Dip, 40–41
  Seafood Paella, 94–95
  Smoked Mackerel
    Kedgeree, 20–21
  Spicy Thai Coconut Shrimp
    Soup, 68
  Summer Rolls, 54
Roasted Salmon with
  Lemon-Garlic Butter, 119
Roasted Sardines with
  Red Peppers and
  Onions, 138
Roasting, 12–13

S
Salads
  Pistachio-Crusted Tuna and
    Lentil Salad, 128–129
  Seared Ahi Tuna Niçoise
    Salad, 36–37
  Shrimp and Orzo Salad, 46
  Shrimp and Papaya
    Salad, 42
  Shrimp Louie, 35
  Smoked Trout and Apple
    Salad, 50
Salmon
  Cioppino, 73–74
  Roasted Salmon with
    Lemon-Garlic Butter, 119
  Salmon Burgers, 71–72
  Salmon Hash with Fried
    Eggs, 26
  Salmon Mousse, 43
  Salmon Teriyaki, 106

Smoked Salmon
  Benedict, 16–17
Smoked Salmon Deviled
  Eggs, 51
Smoked Salmon with Baked
  Eggs in Avocados, 28
Thai-Spiced Salmon Fillet en
  Papillote, 114–115
Sandwiches
  Open-Faced Tuna Melts, 66
  Pan Bagnat (Provençal Tuna
    Sandwiches), 81
  Quick and Easy Oyster Po'
    Boys, 58–59
  Salmon Burgers, 71–72
  Sardine and Pimento
    Bocadillos, 79
  Shrimp Banh Mi
    Sandwiches, 77–78
  Trout Hand Pies, 82–83
Sardines
  Fried Sardines with
    Gremolata, 121–122
  Roasted Sardines with Red
    Peppers and Onions, 138
  Sardine and Pimento
    Bocadillos, 79
Sausage
  Lowcountry Boil, 98
Scallops
  Cioppino, 73–74
  Scallop and Clam Pan
    Roast, 111
  Seared Scallops with
    Pineapple Beurre
    Blanc, 112–113
Seafood. See also Fish; specific
  benefits of consuming, 2
  shopping for, 9–11
  types of, 8–9
Seafood Paella, 94–95
Seared Ahi Tuna Niçoise
  Salad, 36–37

Seared Scallops with Pineapple
  Beurre Blanc, 112–113
Searing, 13
Shellfish, 9
Shrimp
  Bang Bang Shrimp in
    Lettuce Cups, 90
  Bouillabaisse, 75–76
  Broiled Shrimp Scampi with
    Crumbled Bacon, 91
  Chilaquiles with Sautéed
    Shrimp, 30–31
  Chinese Shrimp
    Toast, 52–53
  Cioppino, 73–74
  Classic Creole Shrimp
    Gumbo, 64–65
  Grilled Shrimp Kabobs
    with Pesto
    Sauce, 130–131
  Lowcountry Boil, 98
  Seafood Paella, 94–95
  shopping for, 10
  Shrimp and Orzo
    Salad, 46
  Shrimp and Papaya
    Salad, 42
  Shrimp Banh Mi
    Sandwiches, 77–78
  Shrimp Louie, 35
  Shrimp Omelets, 18–19
  Spicy Thai Coconut Shrimp
    Soup, 68
  Summer Rolls, 54
  Tuna and Tomato
    Frittata, 29
Smoked Mackerel
  Kedgeree, 20–21
Smoked Oyster Soup, 67
Smoked Salmon
  Benedict, 16–17
Smoked Salmon Deviled
  Eggs, 51

Smoked Salmon with Baked
  Eggs in Avocados, 28
Smoked Trout and Apple
  Salad, 50
Smoked Trout and Bacon
  Cornmeal Waffles, 27
Sole Meunière, 107
Soups. *See also* Stews
  Crab Bisque, 62–63
  New England Clam
    Chowder, 60–61
  Smoked Oyster Soup, 67
  Spicy Thai Coconut Shrimp
    Soup, 68
Spaghetti with Clams, 96–97
Spicy Fideos with
  Mussels, 88–89
Spicy Thai Coconut Shrimp
  Soup, 68
Spinach
  Cajun Catfish and Spinach
    Stew, 99
  Oysters
    Rockefeller, 116–117
Squash
  Grilled Shrimp Kabobs with
    Pesto Sauce, 130–131
Squid
  Fried Calamari with Rustic
    Tomato Sauce, 104–105
Steamed Mussels with White
  Wine and Fennel, 110
Steaming, 13
Stews
  Bouillabaisse, 75–76
  Cajun Catfish and Spinach
    Stew, 99
  Cioppino, 73–74
  Classic Creole Shrimp
    Gumbo, 64–65
Summer Rolls, 54
Sustainability, 3, 5

T
Thai-Spiced Salmon Fillet en
  Papillote, 114–115
30-minute
  Bang Bang Shrimp in
    Lettuce Cups, 90
  Blackened Catfish, 108–109
  Broiled Halibut with
    Lemon-Herb
    Persillade, 123
  Broiled Shrimp Scampi with
    Crumbled Bacon, 91
  Crab Rangoons, 47
  Drunken Crab with Garlic
    Fried Rice, 132–133
  Fried Calamari with Rustic
    Tomato Sauce, 104–105
  Fried Sardines with
    Gremolata, 121–122
  Grilled Shrimp Kabobs
    with Pesto
    Sauce, 130–131
  Grilled Tuna Steaks with
    Wasabi Butter, 125
  Macadamia-Crusted
    Mahi-Mahi, 118
  Open-Faced Tuna Melts, 66
  Roasted Sardines with Red
    Peppers and Onions, 138
  Sardine and Pimento
    Bocadillos, 79
  Shrimp Louie, 35
  Shrimp Omelets, 18–19
  Smoked Mackerel
    Kedgeree, 20–21
  Smoked Salmon
    Benedict, 16–17
  Smoked Salmon Deviled
    Eggs, 51
  Smoked Salmon with Baked
    Eggs in Avocados, 28
  Smoked Trout and Apple
    Salad, 50

Sole Meunière, 107
Steamed Mussels with
  White Wine and
  Fennel, 110
Summer Rolls, 54
Tilapia, Jamaican Jerk, with
  Coconut Rice, 136–137
Tomatoes
  Bouillabaisse, 75–76
  Cajun Catfish and Spinach
    Stew, 99
  Chilean Sea Bass with
    Roasted Lemons and
    Fresh Herbs, 92
  Cioppino, 73–74
  Grilled Shrimp Kabobs
    with Pesto
    Sauce, 130–131
  Open-Faced Tuna Melts, 66
  Pan Bagnat (Provençal Tuna
    Sandwiches), 81
  Pistachio-Crusted Tuna and
    Lentil Salad, 128–129
  Quick and Easy Oyster Po'
    Boys, 58–59
  Red Snapper Veracruz, 127
  Sardine and Pimento
    Bocadillos, 79
  Seafood Paella, 94–95
  Seared Ahi Tuna Niçoise
    Salad, 36–37
  Shrimp and Orzo
    Salad, 46
  Smoked Mackerel
    Kedgeree, 20–21
  Spicy Fideos with
    Mussels, 88–89
  Tuna and Tomato
    Frittata, 29
Trout
  Smoked Trout and Apple
    Salad, 50

Trout (*continued*)
    Smoked Trout and Bacon
        Cornmeal Waffles, 27
    Trout Hand Pies, 82–83
Tuna
    Grilled Tuna Steaks with
        Wasabi Butter, 125
    Open-Faced Tuna Melts, 66
    Pan Bagnat (Provençal Tuna
        Sandwiches), 81
    Pistachio-Crusted Tuna and
        Lentil Salad, 128–129
    Seared Ahi Tuna Niçoise
        Salad, 36–37

Tuna and Tomato
    Frittata, 29
Tuna Noodle
    Casserole, 100–101

W

Water chestnuts
    Chinese Shrimp
        Toast, 52–53
Whitefish
    Bouillabaisse, 75–76
    Ceviche, 45

Y

Yogurt
    Bang Bang Shrimp in
        Lettuce Cups, 90
    Salmon Mousse, 43
    Smoked Salmon Deviled
        Eggs, 51

Z

Zucchini
    Grilled Shrimp Kabobs with
        Pesto Sauce, 130–131

ACKNOWLEDGMENTS

With deepest gratitude, I wish to thank Elizabeth, Matt, Daniel, Sara, and the entire production team at Callisto Media for making this book possible.

To my family, I thank them most of all for always being there for me. Their unconditional love and support helps me move forward every day. And thank you to my husband, Paul, for believing in me and letting me follow my dreams. I love you.

ABOUT THE AUTHOR

TERRI DIEN is native New Yorker living in the San Francisco Bay Area. In 2003 she left her career in political consulting to pursue her lifelong passion for cooking and enrolled in City College of San Francisco's Culinary Arts and Hospitality Studies program. She has worked in restaurants in both savory and pastry roles, and has also taught cooking classes for nearly 15 years at Draeger's Cooking School, South San Francisco Parks and Recreation, and Sur La Table. Currently she is Executive Program Chef for Child Care at Google, providing delicious plant-forward meals for children and their educators. Terri lives in San Mateo, California, with her husband, Paul, and their cats Sarah and Henry. Keep in touch by following @ChefTerriDien on Instagram.

9 781641 529181